FORMULA
WIN

YOUR ROAD TO
SUCCESSFUL SELLING

THE INSIDE TRACK

Written by

Andy Ryder & Beat Erb

Contents

"Achieving the results you desire is less about knowing what to do; it is more about doing what you already know"

Andy Ryder

Foreword

by Andy Ryder - The Story of Formula Win
(FWIN Selling)

I remember meeting Beat at a Neuro-Linguistic Programming training in Santa Cruz, California right back in 2006. It was one of those amazing moments in business when you are introduced to someone thinking it'll be a brief 'hello!' and you end up talking for hours! We discovered that not only did we have similar backgrounds in engineering and international sales but that we also shared a fascination for human behavior. At the time it was unusual for me to meet someone with whom I could converse about all those topics at once!

The icing on the cake for me, however, was learning that Beat and I shared a common mission that was to bridge the gap between the rational and emotional sides of selling. While delivering sales and leadership training to clients around the world, I had been thinking about it quietly for many years and suddenly there was someone on the same page! We were aligned in our thinking that both rational and emotional elements were crucial to successful selling but had yet to discover anyone in the field who was talking about it in quite the same way.

We clarified our thinking and little did we know at the time, we were putting together the foundations of a book, the one that you are holding in your hands today. He brought much needed organization, international sales management experience and clarity to my thoughts and writing process. Beat added the pivotal methodology for collecting and presenting information to clients, now known as the FWIN Clipboard.

Fast-forward to the present day and our winning strategy has been translated by one of our clients into 13 languages. As it developed over the years, the strategy has helped salespeople all over the world to win new clients. In addition, it has helped to establish and enhance relationships with new as well as existing customers. Time and again customers tell us that its practical application has increased sales.

Formula Win methodology – as it has come to be known – has evolved into a skills training that can be used across all industries in a Business-to-Business (B2B) setting. It is a fully rounded methodology based on three distinct aspects of selling:

» Firstly, the techniques needed to become a valued business partner (The Inside Track)
» Secondly, how to communicate value to the right people (The Qualifying Lap)
» Thirdly, how to plan and manage an ever-changing pipeline (Winning the Circuit)

The structure of this book brings together the emotional and rational approaches of selling in today's complex digital and analogue world. It will guide you to a more structured and conscious approach to your communication skills in sales and, when applied, will take you on a journey with your clients that is enjoyable, authentic and mutually beneficial.

The key however, is in the word 'application'. For the sales methods Beat and I are introducing here to work, they have to be put into practice. Knowing salespeople as we do, we understand that sometimes there is a tendency to fall into old patterns and habits. So, we invite you not only to read this book but to commit to 'putting learning into practice', thereby following in the footsteps of so many successful sales professionals who are now using FWIN methodology in their working lives.

It has been a true joy to bring all of this together into a book, which we know has the potential to change so many salespeople's lives for the better.

I hope you enjoy reading it as much as we have enjoyed writing it.

Andy Ryder
Co-author of Formula Win Selling

Acknowledgements

This book is the product of conversations between two men who share a passion for sales and if it wasn't for the hard work, dedication and support of some amazing people we wouldn't be able to share it with you. Therefore we would like to start by thanking our teachers, guides and colleagues with whom we have worked and developed ideas over the years, specifically Andi Roberts and Debi Garrod who were part of the initial editing, Hywel Griffith for his fastidious approach to the direction and production of training videos for our clients and Dr BJ Fogg, founder of the Behavior Design Lab at Stanford University, USA whose work on Tiny Habits® has provided the backbone for putting this learning into daily practice.

Formula Win has been brought to life by the cover artwork, graphics and illustrations of deuce:studio and whispercreative, as well as by Amber Beardmore's thorough and detailed investigation of our material, her research and her gentle yet robust challenging of our ideas.

Finally, we would like to express our deepest thanks to Ann Lowe, whose indefatigable and ongoing support with written content, coaching us through the publishing process and reading of initial drafts has been instrumental in getting this project completed. Also to Mary Turner Thomson for putting the final touches to the layout.

How to use this book

To get the best results out of this book we suggest you read it alongside a 'buddy', or as we like to call them your 'Co-Driver'. This is someone who is as motivated as you are to improve their sales performance. Read a chapter and practice imaginary scenarios in a café or online, based on real clients, together. Then after using the techniques in real life, re-group and go to other parts of the book where you feel you need to up your game. Remember, after every session with your co-driver to think about the type of spark/ reminder you will use to remind you to make the technique a habit – and then, DO IT!

The stakes in sales and sales training are high!

Let us begin by asking ourselves three simple questions:

1. 'Would a racing car driver jump into a car capable of over 200 mph, leaving the results of their actions to trial (and possibly fatal) error?'
2. 'How often are sales professionals left without training and a consistent methodology to follow?'
3. 'What is the impact of salespeople 'practicing' new approaches on real, prospective customers?'

A number of our workshop participants were all too familiar with the scenarios above. Whether you are experienced and you have an underlying feeling that something is missing in your box of communication tools or you are new to sales, we offer you a methodology to work with that's quick, easy and light!

Many told us they had been working in sales for a while and although they were good at their jobs, their employers had given them very little formal training. Some were struggling to give the 'WOW factor' to their customers when pitching for new business. They knew there was more they could do to understand their customers from the outset but after some recent failures they didn't know where to turn. Some were attending customer meetings feeling increasingly disorganized and a little out of their depth. We all know the anxious feeling that missing a sales target can cause!

Fast-forward a few short months and a number of international salespeople who stood in front of us after learning the FWIN Selling techniques, are now energized and organized. Not only that but some feel that they can even switch from their sales support and business development roles to selling on the front line.

One of our favorites, Julie from the UK said she was enjoying incredible success, building trusting customer relationships by applying the simple techniques introduced in this book. She also wished us well with the publication and said, 'if it's even half as good as the face-to-face training it will be a great success, I'm sure.'

If you've picked up FWIN Selling, it is likely that you are someone who feels there is more you could be doing to give yourself that competitive edge. You may even be new to selling and keen to start out on the right foot with a structure and clear roadmap to success.

Formula Win Selling is going to show you how to perform at the top of your game in **all** your customer interactions.

I (Andy) first became interested in helping people improve their success in sales after being dropped in at the deep end myself in the early 2000s. I'd landed a role in sales almost by accident and suddenly found myself pitching to huge companies, with little structure or guidance on how to succeed. I was tasked with establishing a sales organization in a foreign country. Our fees were 2-3 times higher than the local competition and I was working in an industry that was completely new to me.

Over time, I began to realize that there are three keys to successful selling: understanding your customer's business, qualifying mutual opportunities and closing deals ahead of stiff competition. I set about creating a methodology to share with others, so that they did not have to go through the same steep learning curve as I did. You, the reader, will benefit hugely from the hindsight, highlights and horror stories, which my co-author Beat and I bring from this experience.

Combined, we have spent almost 50 years working in sales and sales training environments. We have written this book to minimize the pain of those who often feel that they have been dropped in the 'sales deep end' without the necessary lifeboat, support, or structure to perform as well as they know they can.

This book is the first of a trilogy. **The Inside Track** focuses on how to position yourself as a valued business partner through a series of techniques designed to give you the competitive edge when interacting with prospects and customers. In the second book **The Qualifying Lap**, you will learn how to deliver inspiring value messages that keep the conversation away from price and firmly focused on what you are offering. The third book – **Winning the Circuit** provides you with the key to planning and managing your sales pipeline and territories, so that you and your team can effectively meet your sales targets ahead of the competition.

Each book, however, revolves around one central theme: *"if you always do what you always did, you will always get what you always got."* You may have heard the expression before – but how often do you do anything differently after only hearing it or reading it? Therein lies the difference, after 'experiencing' Formula Win Selling with your co-driver, you will do things differently and you will achieve even better results!

Transforming your approach to sales takes dedication and over time this becomes habit. The same way that other tweaks to what we do eventually become the way we do things.

If you want to give your customers insights, to educate, challenge them and ultimately add value, then you will benefit from:

» Having a SOLID STRUCTURE to FIND, WIN & KEEP clients, which is easily replicated as a successful best practice.
» Being consistent in your behavior – by DOING WHAT YOU LEARN.
» Using a high degree of Emotional Intelligence and INTERPERSONAL SKILLS to leverage communications with you and with others.

During the last twenty years of teaching sales techniques we have heard sellers openly express the wish to refresh their fundamental selling skills. They say that *"if you get the basics right, everything else follows."* However, when following up on their progress, we often find that if they have not practiced their learning with repetition and regular coaching, the opportunity for change is very quickly lost. It is so easy to return to the status quo. To return to what they have always done.

To help you turn the techniques from this book into actual habits, we have provided a short insight into habit-forming in the appendix. After each chapter, we recommend you refer to this and focus on making the learning stick by forming new habits.

Should you wish to know more about this innovative method, you may want to look at the work of Behavior Scientist from Stanford by Dr BJ Fogg.

Another reason for writing FWIN Selling is our vision to refresh and to rejuvenate experienced sales professionals by helping you to:

» Enjoy your everyday work – remembering that people still buy from people
» Convert experience and FWIN knowledge into successful daily practice
» Connect your work in sales with meaningful purpose of service to others
» Sell more!

Introduction

We begin with the first of three vital circuits that we call The Inside Track.

The Inside Track is what sellers actually do when interacting, either face to face or virtually, with the people we call customers. It is all about giving you, the salesperson, the competitive advantage.

Although, the phrase 'Inside Track' originally hails from horse racing and describes the inner or shorter track of a course on which it is easier to win. Its connotation in journalism perfectly fits with Formula Win Selling, as it gives you that edge, that scoop, that exclusive information that your competitor is lacking.

As a salesperson, you gain competitive advantage by having one – or indeed many conversations with your prospective customers. These could be formally scheduled meetings or ad hoc calls. Such interactions enable you to gain insight beyond what is immediately knowable from research or journals. There are, of course, other ways you can acquire a strategic advantage (we explore these in much greater detail later in the FWIN series in *Winning the Circuit*). However, for the purpose of this book, we focus primarily on gaining vital information through conversations and interactions with your customer or prospect.

By observing the most successful salespeople in action, we have noticed that interactions – though they may differ in content – almost always follow a pattern. You as the salesperson introduce yourself, ask questions, listen to the customer's needs and ultimately suggest a solution (that you have for sale).

Applied systematically, The Inside Track offers a series of techniques that help you to build that buyer-seller relationship. It takes you on a journey from a first-time meeting with a person, known in the field of sales as a 'Prospect' – right through to closing the deal. It will show you how to repeatedly close deals with that same person, who in time can become a loyal customer and in many cases, a friend.

When used regularly, The Inside Track will bring joy and a healthy interest in human communication skills to the work of sales, as it helps it to make the whole process feel effortless.

The Formula Win Metaphor

As mentioned earlier, we liken an FWIN salesperson to a racing car driver, travelling at speeds of over 200 mph. This skill requires discipline, full concentration and an accurate understanding of everything going on around them. Total awareness of how others are acting on the circuit is essential to winning, as is an appreciation of the weather conditions. There is a lot to consider and a lot going on and while the 'autopilot' can get a car around the circuit, it is the skilled and focused human driver who brings perception and awareness into the equation ensuring that they are more likely to win the race.

Introducing 'Sparks'

Due to the busy lives we all lead and the increasing number of distractions from all directions, it's so easy for us to forget our daily training, however minor the effort needed might be. The FWIN reminders to help you stick to the new techniques and the acronyms are called Sparks - you may be relieved to learn that they are already located in your car:

» Your **B.R.A.K.E** can remind you to slow down with customers and listen

» A glance at your **TEMPERATURE GAUGE** can be the simple reminder needed to stay hydrated and to take more care of yourself

» Finally, a 5-speed gear shift is the way to **D.R.I.V.E** when asking questions

We will of course introduce you to the concepts of B.R.A.K.E and D.R.I.V.E later in this book!

Locating Sparks in your car

Many, if not all, salespeople D.R.I.V.E cars (even those based in the city, will probably use one at the weekends). For many of us, our car is the space where we talk to ourselves daily, about everything from other drivers to that next client visit and the all-consuming sales target for the month.

It is where we sit, driving home in the evening while mulling over what we saw, what we heard and how we felt during the day. It is where we may even start rehearsing what we will do tomorrow or on Monday morning.

So, what better place to link reminders – Sparks – to the reality of moving sales opportunities along?

Your car can become the place where many ideas, dreams or new selling skills are 'sparked' into reality!

The FORMULA WIN mindset

Racing car drivers are always trying to find the most efficient and safest way around a circuit. This involves a considerable amount of trial and error at every stage and drivers continually learn new methods, even during the last lap of a race.

Speed efficiency (use of time) is almost an art form. It's like being a tightrope walker: even if the rope stretches across the same two points, you'll never walk it the same way twice. Winning is a balancing act: every car is different due to the tuning, the design, or the track conditions.

Likewise, every potential customer is different. The drivers that stand out are those who are quickest to adapt to changing conditions and to respond accordingly, just like the salesperson who confidently makes a counteroffer when the competition is closing in.

As in the world of racing, conditions in the business world are constantly changing. We liken rainy conditions – known in motor sport as The Great Equalizer – to a procurement process which attempts to reduce the seller's offer to a mere commodity by obscuring its unique value to a decision based solely on price. In this instance, it is only the skills of the seller that can overcome such conditions and still win the race. The driver's knowledge of the circuit is comparable to that of the seller understanding the client's business needs, priorities, decision makers, competition and product position in today's market.

To grow as a world-class driver or as a professional seller, it is essential to adopt the mindset of self-awareness and openness to feedback. While the driver constantly monitors telemetry and video in order to improve, salespeople plan and observe customer behavior and sales pipelines, which contribute to a structured and winning sales approach. Sellers also learn psychology-based models to help understand human behavior and to hone their communication skills to win the client's trust.

The ultimate comparison of the racing car driver and a sales professional is adaptability. A driver choosing the fastest line on ever-degrading tires while coping with the pressure of competition from behind formulates new strategies and calculations in the moment. These all compare to a salesperson's agility when engaging with customers in an ever-increasing and competitive market. With the right skills and plenty of practice, the sales professional is also agile enough to manoeuvre through the sales call with a client.

The Winning Formula

Behind every successful performance – whether it is sport, music or painting a picture – there is a disciplined structure and technique to success. In high-performance sales scenarios, this structure comprises THE ART and THE SCIENCE of selling.

The art is reflected by salespeople who can read and influence clients. They perform better than those who cannot, as the human connection is still key even in today's technological world. On the other hand, the science of selling is something quite different. It is about being organized following a consistent process. The seller who forgets to enter data into the CRM or does not read the customer's annual report will fail to demonstrate the required professionalism that the client expects.

FWIN methodology blends both the art and the science of selling to create well-rounded and dependable sales results. However, one thing which cannot be stressed enough is that this formula can only succeed when it is put into practice in real life. After all here is a 100% chance that when you use different techniques, such as these, with your clients, you will be sure to get different results.

Your Co-Driver for the FWIN journey

Practicing with a friendly colleague – we use the term co-driver to describe such a person – is undeniably less daunting and less risky than meeting with a real client! Therefore, throughout the book we will invite you to work with a trusted person to test out the new techniques you are learning. As you reflect, you will begin to understand a lot more about yourself, your clients and your competitors. You and your co-driver will experience learning and change together. What's more, you can rely on each other to ensure accountability, enjoyment and reward.

If you want to stop smoking, to train for a marathon, or to bring up a family, you are more likely to succeed when you feel emotionally committed and accountable to your partner. Relying on each other creates a safe environment of trust and mutual benefit as well as sustaining momentum and accountability to push on.

What's more, when something that we expect to happen doesn't, if we're in a safe environment, we can reflect, test assumptions and adapt theories. We can remember and learn from that experience. It is this process which allows us to become consciously aware of any changes which we can make next time. By practicing scenarios as in the Pitstops, this learning is embedded for you to choose as a new and successful habit.

Choosing your Co-Driver

Find someone who is as motivated as you are to learn and to perform. Someone whose opinion you trust. Preferably, they will be reading this book at the same pace as you. Ideally, you want to work with someone who motivates you to do better (and vice versa) but who is not going to see the work as competitive between you.

You're looking for mutually supportive collaboration whereby you can share honest feedback as well as a desire to win!

Practice. Practice. Practice.

Just as every professional sports person benefits from thousands of hours of practice, Formula Win sellers achieve their targets by developing new habits – also known as unconscious competencies.

These new skills are the result of neurological pathways that are strengthened through discussion and repetition.

You'll notice throughout the book that we recommend some Pitstops. These Pitstops are your opportunity to begin to practice and reflect on what you're learning. As you work through, you may notice that each Pitstop follows a 3-step learning routine:

» **EXPERIENCE** the feeling of nerves, improvement and enjoyment
» **LEARN** performance-enhancing habits by role-playing a chosen best practice
» **PERFORM** with real clients and report back to your co-driver afterwards

EXPERIENCE   **LEARN**   **PERFORM**

People (still) buy from People

1

Business is all about people... even in the world of the Internet, the final decision for any sale is made by a person. As has always been the case in selling, building a relationship with this person is vital.

Wheels of Relationship

The metaphor we use to describe this process is called the Wheels of Relationship and it is illustrated by the chassis of a vehicle that needs four wheels to function:

1. Rapport
2. Understanding
3. Trust
4. Value

While the four wheels are crucial, the order in which you assemble them onto the chassis is equally vital to your outcome.

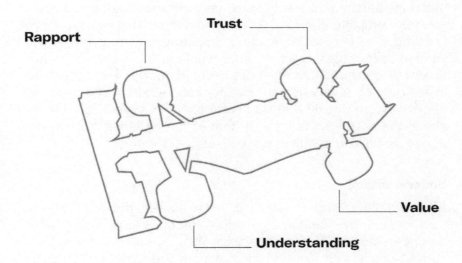

Rapport

Trust

Value

Understanding

The seller's goal is to earn the right to converse with the customer about their understanding of value, without falling into the common default position of discussing price. Once you have established a modicum of rapport, the quality of your questions will demonstrate your eagerness to comprehend your customer's ultimate business goals, needs and challenges. Showing this understanding will ultimately win you the trust needed to open the door to a conversation about both the expected value and that which you provide.

When assembled in the correct order you achieve that all-important sense of alignment. Here, the dynamic of the relationship shifts and the client acknowledges the benefits of you as a trusted partner and the value of your products and services.

To build this well-oiled and reliable machine, let us look more closely at each of the wheels of relationship.

Assembling the Wheels of Relationship

Rapport

The first element in building the client-seller relationship is Rapport. Rapport originates from a French word used to describe the harmony achieved between two people through communication. It is a natural human phenomenon that we achieve by simply connecting with another person. Perhaps you can remember meeting a person, whether in a business context or otherwise, when you felt completely at ease in their presence. This was evidence that you were in rapport. In such a meeting, you may have found yourself mirroring the words and even the body language they used. Mirroring and finding things in common with another person arises out of our very human need for connection. As humans, we know subconsciously that it is safer to be in a group than to be alone. We achieve this type of connection by being alert to the things we have in common with the people we meet.

Understanding

After building Rapport, you will have earned the right to ask your prospective customer a series of questions to establish an understanding of their business, their overall goals and their current challenges. You will also explore the factors driving the customer to invest, in order to fulfil their needs. The way to achieve this and to improve your credibility is by asking relevant questions about the customer's business by using the FWIN D.R.I.V.E and Clipboard techniques. You must demonstrate a selfless yearning to put yourself in the client's shoes and fully comprehend the bigger picture, facts and implications of what the customer wishes to achieve.

Trust

When the customer feels that you have an accurate and empathic understanding of their situation and that your first and foremost interest is to help them, they begin to trust you. This trust opens the relationship and allows for the dialogue to move away from the organization's business needs towards a more emotional interaction. Once this trusting connection is established, you can introduce the value of your products and services both in logical/ numerical and intangible terms. In other words, you can move the conversation towards a dialogue about value only after rapport and understanding have been established.

Value

"With marketplaces and the internet filled with offerings, you know that you very often can only win deals that are based on value and not on price". The Harvard Business Review, for example, contends that value propositions can make a significant contribution to business strategy and performance.[1]

There are two immediate perceptions of value:

1. ***Quantitative (economic) value*** appeals to the logical side of the sale. For example, a computer system crash of a medium-sized supermarket has been estimated to cost $200,000 per hour. By preventing just one possible crash per year, the seller saves the customer $200,000 with their offering. The same can be said for any investment made in any industry where a clear numerical value is calculable.

---

1 James, A., Narus, J & van Rossum, W. (2006. Customer value propositions in business markets. Harvard Business Review, 84(3), 1-10.

2. **It pays to know what else matters to the customer.** Value that you can explain to the customer in the absence of numbers, revenue or cost savings is known as qualitative value. Such value can include a better reputation, enhanced brand value or increased employee engagement. Very often services such as training or consulting fall into this category, as they depend on so many factors that have no direct link to a tangible monetary value.

3. **In our experience, it is worth investing time in finding both the Quantitative as well as the Qualitative Value**, as they help the customer understand the more subtle, yet important reasons to invest in your solution and logically justify a purchase.

Many factors can have a direct impact on value. We go into more detail on how to calculate value on The Qualifying Lap (Reference: FWIN Book 2 – The Qualifying Lap).

Since customers often remain focused on price, many salespeople never get to talk about the value their products and services. From our perspective, this is a lose-lose situation: salespeople run the risk of leaving a lot of money on the table, while simultaneously customers are left unaware of the value they could receive. In this scenario, the customer settles on a cheaper solution centred on a price-based decision rather than a cost-effective one based on value.

Conversely, by moving the conversation away from features, functions and price to a value-based discussion, you communicate on a more partner-like rather than vendor-like level. Meaning, that both you and your customer are able to gain a mutual Inside Track!

4. **Personal versus Professional Value – What's in it for me?** As well as the quantitative and qualitative ideas around value we cannot ignore the human element. *"An oft-overlooked factor is what the buyer stands to gain (or lose) from the purchase personally – they're almost 50% more likely to buy when there's something in it for them."* [2]

---

2 *Nathan, S., & Schmidt, K. (2013). Promotion to Emotion: Connecting B2B Customers to Brands.*

The Customer's Experience

Nowadays, an ever-increasing amount of advertising is pumped out to customers through a variety of digital and social media channels. More than ever before, buyers need experts to help them decipher what is the best value and in some cases to help communicate this value to their higher-level decision makers and executives in the customer's organization.

» 76 percent of B2B buyers still find it helpful to talk to salespeople for first time purchases (McKinsey).[3]

» 75 percent of consumers will still choose to interact with a real person even as the technology for automated solutions improves (PwC).[4]

Research shows that to gain the 'Inside Track' (a competitive advantage) with any customer, the salesperson should focus primarily on the customer's buying experience. A positive experience as a customer directly affects whether they will buy and whether they will repeat business: *"Cx (Customer experience) is huge – 96% of buyers said this affects whether they buy from a vendor again."*[5]

To help you do this, we'd like you to remember that as well as being a salesperson, you also have a vast experience of being a customer.

Reflect on your own purchasing experiences for a moment.

In doing so, you might agree that it is the person you buy from rather than the product that influences your purchasing choices. This means that as a buyer, you can change your perception of a product or service based on your overall experience with that one salesperson. That is incredibly powerful information when you shift back into the role of a salesperson.

The FWIN Inside Track focuses on the client's journey, not that of the seller. While you plan the journey, it is the passenger (the client) who decides whether or not to continue. Therefore, how

---

3   Angevine, C., Plotkin, C. L., & Stanley, J. (2017). When B2B buyers want to go digital–and when they don't. McKinsey Quarterly, 8, 12-15.

4   PwC (2018). Future of Customer Experience Survey 2017/18. PwC. Retrieved 22 August 2021

5   Demand Gen Report (2018). 2018 Content Preferences Survey Report. Retrieved 22 August 2021

you behave, think and act will determine whether the buyer feels your products and services are the best investment for them.

The seller's mindset

As in every successful human achievement, a certain mindset is key to achieving the end goal and beating the competition. The FWIN Customer Experience is based on the following seller's mindset:

*"I am here to find out all about **your needs ... This conversation is about you!** Not me."*

*"I can only offer you my product or service when I am sure that I **understand** your business, your needs and the fit provided by my solution."*

A skillful balance between asking and telling customers enables you to create a client experience that is both assuring and persuasive. Putting elements of the Inside Track into practice during your client interactions ensures that you enjoy increased success in selling.

Structure - An Organized Approach

When we ask corporate customers why they decided to buy a certain product or service, they often respond by telling us how they felt about the seller. They describe successful salespeople as having the following traits:

Structured - Confident - Collaborative - Knowledgeable

Competent - In Control

To help you achieve these six key traits of successful sales professionals, we have designed Formula Win Selling around three main circuits that lead to the finish line. In this book, we focus on customer-facing-skills on 'The Inside Track', before taking a more strategic approach in The Qualifying Lap, Winning the Circuit and The Finish Line.

The Inside Track Structure

As you learn to use the structure and techniques on the Inside Track, you will see how the traits described influence the customer's perception of you and your company and crucially, how to embody them to ensure your ongoing success.

We believe that a memorable and successful Customer Experience results from a journey planned and executed by a professional salesperson. We have observed this journey in various sales interactions, in different countries, across many industries. When we modelled it, we found that it is built on several, often unconscious steps. These steps form what we call The Inside Track and are illustrated by the chevrons below.

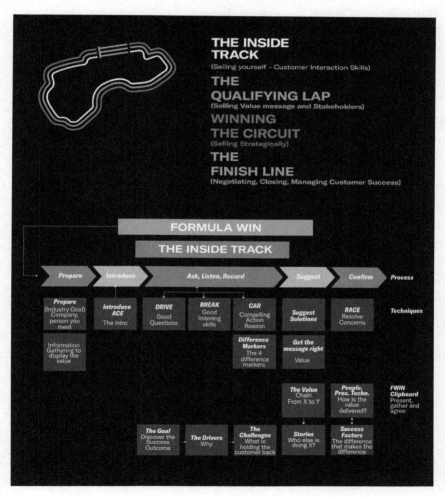

THE INSIDE TRACK
(Selling yourself - Customer Interaction Skills)

THE QUALIFYING LAP
(Selling Value message and Stakeholders)

WINNING THE CIRCUIT
(Selling Strategically)

THE FINISH LINE
(Negotiating, Closing, Managing Customer Success)

FORMULA WIN

THE INSIDE TRACK

Prepare → Introduce → Ask, Listen, Record → Suggest → Confirm → Process

| Prepare (Industry Goal) Company, person you meet | Introduce ACE The intro | DRIVE Good Questions | BREAK Good listening skills | CAR Compelling Action Reason | Suggest Solutions | RACE Resolve Concerns | Techniques |

Information Gathering to display the value

Difference Markers The 4 difference markers

Get the message right Value

The Value Chain From X to Y

People, Proc. Techn. How is the value delivered?

FWIN Clipboard Present, gather and agree

The Goal Discover the Success Outcome → **The Drivers** Why → **The Challenges** What is holding the customer back → **Stories** Who else is doing it? → **Success Factors** The difference that makes the difference

In summary

In your role as a salesperson, you are constantly interacting with customers on the Inside Track.

Your primary goals are to understand your customer's needs, how their decision-making process will lead to a successful sale while winning THEIR TRUST and permission to talk about YOUR VALUE.

A good customer relationship works best when the following happen:

» Rapport is established
» A common Understanding reached
» Trust is gained
» The Value is understood and accepted by the customer.

In other words, all four wheels are firmly fitted onto the chassis.

Customer relationships based on this foundation can and do, last long into the future, providing mutual benefits to both customers and salespeople alike. We will talk more about the concept of mutual 'value' in our next book in the series called The Qualifying Lap, where we provide more guidance on bringing value to the forefront of the customer conversation.

To begin the Formula Win series, we have written this first book solely on the subject most salespeople relate to best – meeting customers! Whether online or face-to-face, sellers agree that gaining 'The Inside Track' is the most direct route to closing a sale or disengaging from a potential opportunity (and therefore saving resources).

How to gain the Inside Track

How much more revenue is possible when:

1. You prepare and structure your communication from opening to closing a deal?
2. You slow down and truly listen?
3. You resolve customers' 'concerns' rather than handling 'objections'?

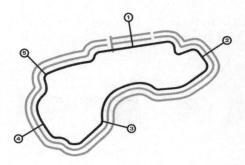

THE INSIDE TRACK

1. Prepare
2. Introduce
3. Ask, Listen, Record
4. Suggest
5. Confirm

Getting 'on track' with your customer

How The Inside Track helps you to align and to stay aligned with your customer in three different types of customer interactions. How to stay 'on the same track'.

Interactions with your customers will vary depending on where they are in their buying process. To be aligned with your customer and to ensure that you are both on the same track, you must adapt your approach to each interaction or sales call (for simplicity, we will be using the term 'sales call' to describe any direct communication with a customer or potential customer).

Your approach will depend on:

» How long you and the customer have known one another
» Whether the meeting is early or late in the customer's decision-making process
» How many representatives from the customer's organization are involved
» The reason for the meeting, for example, is to discover needs to align with the customer's colleagues and manager's needs, or to make a final presentation of the proposed solution
» The value of the potential sale and resources needed to close a deal

To help you adjust your actions on The Inside Track, we associate the type of sales call with the customer's position on their buying decision timeline and with your intention for this particular call. For example, a Discovery Call, an Alignment Call or a Closing Call.

Let's look at each type of call in more detail.

1. The Discovery Call

The Discovery call is an initial meeting with a new client, or with a client who has new needs and challenges with which you are able to help.

In the early stages of a client engagement, your goal is to discover:

» The customer's situation and perceived needs
» What drives the customer towards investment and which roadblocks impede their success
» The customer's unique perception of value
» Whether this is beneficial for the customer and for you - is it a real opportunity for both parties?

When your relationship with a customer is new, as mentioned in the 'wheels of relationship', you seek to establish a connection of mutual trust and value with the client. Your authenticity and true intention to provide value will create that bond and will allow you to discover the important insights listed above.

2. The Value Alignment Call

The Value Alignment call is a follow-up call with a client who you meet for a second, third or fourth time. The goal is to ensure that you, the client and any other stakeholders all have the same understanding of the needs and challenges.

As you meet more than one influencer in the client organization, you seek to reach mutual understanding and support for a possible fit between the needs, the solution and the expected value by all of the stakeholders.

As well as by adding increased value to the solution, this search for synergies and support across a wider range of influencers puts you into a stronger lobbying position that increases your ability to close the deal when the final decision is being made.

In a Value Alignment call, you work with your customer's internal stakeholders and influencers to explore and to demonstrate whether the Quantitative and Qualitative Value of your products and services are a good investment for your client to help them achieve their goals.

3. The Closing Call

In a Closing call, your primary goal is to focus on a final presentation with the decision makers to sign the contract.

Your aim is to close the deal and to gain a final agreement for the customer to purchase their products and services at a price where they get the best value for what they spend. This is not necessarily the lowest price.

To help you achieve your goals in each of the three types of sales calls mentioned above, you will adapt each of the models and techniques contained in the five chevrons.

Based on where the customer is in the buying process, you are free to choose your approach to each of the five chevrons.

Prepare – to win!

In the **Prepare** phase, you can research the customer and their business in a variety of ways, ranging from using the internet, to gaining insight from personal contacts. The goal is to know enough so that you can ask knowledgeable questions at a meeting. The act of asking such informed questions demonstrates that you have done your homework, as well as help to build rapport and trust.

In every type of sales call it is advisable to pay particular attention to preparing an introduction that sets the scene for the meeting. The A.C.E model will show you how to do this in three simple steps.

You can also prepare any necessary materials to bring to the meeting or to send to the customer in advance by email.

Here is a quick summary of what you must prepare in the different types of sales calls:

Discovery Call – 'Prepare'

Read the client's annual report, website as well as industry journals. Speak with colleagues. Research from the internet.

Alignment Call – 'Prepare'

Compare what you know about the customer's situation with possible products and solutions from your company that you know will work. It pays to know what matters to the customer. The criteria for making a purchase decision may not be solely influenced by the needs of the company. How often when meeting customers and other stakeholders do we learn about more personal drivers, such as the need to be 'seen' at a reputable conference or have their name 'heard' in the boardroom?

Prepare   Introduce   Ask, Listen,

Since research from *Salesforce* tells that 72% of customers will share their good experiences with others[1], why not help this along by sharing some real success stories of your own?

Closing Call – 'Prepare'

Prepare the FWIN Seven Step Value Message which shows how your suggested investment matches perfectly with the customer's needs. You will find how to build the 'Seven Step Value Message'.

Introduce – the ACE up your sleeve!

Here, you focus on those initial, opening words which you will say to the customer. You might 'never get a second chance to make a first impression' and therefore it is crucial that you adapt your introduction to the situation. Be sure to bear in mind any existing relationship with the customer. Your goal is to open the door to a meeting in which the customer feels they will get good value and will make the best use of their time. The introduction also helps both parties agree on expectations that they can measure retrospectively.

Every interaction with a client begins with an introduction of some sort. The adaptation of this introduction to the specific sales phase and the individual client should be customized as well as authentic.

Discovery call – 'Introduce'

In the Discovery call, you introduce yourself and your company with a statement that promises the customer high value and a good return on the time they invest with you. Be clear about your expectation for this meeting, to gather and share information in order to discover whether your products and services can benefit them. Your focus is to discover as much information as possible to

---

1   McGinnis, D. (2019). Customer Service Statistics and Trends. Retrieved 22 August 2021

Record > Suggest > Confirm

calculate the Quantitative and Qualitative Value of your products and Services.

Alignment call – 'Introduce'

In an Alignment Call, you inform the customer about the actions you took since the last interaction that you had with them. You take a deeper look on how your products or services are aligned with the customer's needs.

Closing call – 'Introduce'

Impress the customer with the high level of insight you have gathered. Explain to the decision makers that this meeting is for them to feel confident in signing the contract and engage you and your company in the work that needs doing. The presentation of the solution will start with a bold statement that holds the customer's attention until you can show how your unique offering will achieve their Ultimate Success Outcome.

Ask, Listen, Record – interactively

In the Ask, Listen, Record chevron, you use different questioning techniques to record and share information with your customer.

Your goal is to make the experience as interactive as possible. This interaction is critical in building and maintaining rapport while building trust in the relationship.

The ability to adapt this chevron to the situation derives mostly from you actively listening to the customer and enabling the conversation to flow. Your dialogue is, as always, adapted to the specific sales phase you are in at that time with the customer.

The acronyms you see in the descriptions below will all be described when we take a more detailed look at the specific behaviors required for each.

Discovery Call – 'Ask, Listen, Record'

Ask (D.R.I.V.E), Listen (B.R.A.K.E), Record (FWIN Clipboard) from the customer about their goals, needs and challenges. Engage the customer by finding the drivers behind their company's investments (collect information to calculate quantitative and qualitative value) and about the challenges they are facing in achieving their Ultimate Success Outcome.

Alignment Call – 'Ask, Listen, Record'

Compare what you know about the customer's situation and

possible options which your customer may have already begun to explore. As part of an Alignment Call, you test if and to what extent the Quantitative and Qualitative Value of your products and services is understood and accepted by the customer.

Closing Call – 'Ask, Listen, Record'

Verify the information on which you have based your offer. Explain the value of this offer and how your unique solution helps the customers like no other can.

Suggest – what to do next

If the call has gone to plan, suggest your pre-planned next step. However, this is real life and not every call does go to plan. You may need to adapt your suggestion in line with what you discover along the way. The main objective – and a measure of success for you – is that when the customer agrees with your next suggested action, it moves you closer to addressing the customer's challenges and therefore, closing the deal.

During the additional phases of the customer's journey, the content of Suggest is adapted according to the related sales phase. A word of caution, however: you may have to stop yourself from trying too hard to sell. Be careful not to turn a discovery call into a closing call. You will lose any rapport and trust already built with the customer. A professional salesperson is patient.

Remember: the most successful sellers don't sell. They create situations where customers want to buy from them!

Discovery call - 'Suggest'

Here, you could suggest coming back with more insight based on the information you gathered during the Discovery call. Alternatively, you could suggest a visit for them to meet another of your satisfied customers. According to referral marketing statistics, referred customers have a 37% higher customer retention rate[2] and 64% of buyers said peer reviews and feedback are what hold most sway with them. What's more, B2B companies with referrals experience a 70% higher conversion rate.[3]

Alignment call - 'Suggest'

During the Alignment call, you can test the Quantitative and Qualitative value of potential products and services for different influencers and clarify any outstanding questions. You might want to suggest sharing this value with your customer's colleagues to enhance support for your solution.

Closing call – 'Suggest'

In the Closing call, suggest how your customer can move from their current situation to an improved situation by getting value from your solution along the Value Journey. Be sure to use the client's language here. Show your customer **Quantitative and Qualitative Value**. Using relevant reference cases, you show that it already works.

Confirm – the icing on the cake!

In the **Discovery, Alignment and Closing** phases, the Confirm chevron requires that you summarize the main points of the meeting, noting any future actions that both you and the customer have agreed to undertake.

---

2   Newman, D. (2015). Love It Or Hate It: Influencer Marketing Works. Retrieved 22 August 2021
3   Demand Gen Report (2018). 2018 Content Preferences Survey Report. Retrieved 22 August 2021

Your goal is to confirm and underpin your credibility while at the same time instilling confidence in the customer that the ongoing relationship will be of benefit for both parties.

The Confirm chevron leaves the customer with positive answers to two key questions:

1. **Why** choose you and your company?
2. **What** are the necessary next steps to achieve the client's goals?

We will explore each of these steps in more detail and introduce practical techniques that you can utilize to close your deal successfully. These exercises (known as Pitstops) will help you practice the techniques in preparation for your real customer meetings.

In summary

As in most successful enterprises, a structured and repeatable approach is the basis of a winning formula.

However, too much structure can cramp the style and unique qualities of any skilled communicator. Therefore, it must be flexible enough to accommodate a variety of different scenarios. In the case of meeting potential and existing customers, the three key scenarios revolve around engaging customers in one or more of three different types of sales interaction or sales call.

1. Discovery Call
2. Alignment Call
3. Closing Call

The Formula Win 'Clipboard'

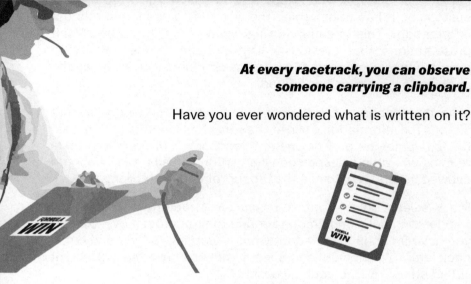

At every racetrack, you can observe someone carrying a clipboard.

Have you ever wondered what is written on it?

At Formula Win Selling, the FWIN Clipboard is used to capture the vital information needed to 'Win the Race'. This includes the strategy and other crucial information that hopefully the competition may not have. The Clipboard is fundamental to bringing you to the finish line ahead of the competition. As you begin to work with it, you will see that it becomes a constant companion giving you a structure that keeps you on the Inside Track.

In one of his previous jobs, Beat was looking for a good way to give salespeople a structure to ensure they had the flexibility to interact with the customer while capturing the necessary information to calculate quantitative and qualitative value. Once he found the methodology, it was quickly included in the education curriculum for all business partners and it was taught at every one of his company's educational events.

Some of the partners that he and his team taught made the methodology their own and fundamentally changed their way of selling (with great success). On the other hand, other partners used it as a structure in the background.

For the salespeople who adopted it and used it in front of their customers, it has transformed the way they present and capture information. This means moving away from the PowerPoint presentations that previously limited them in their ability to simultaneously present and discuss solutions. Over time, the methodology was further refined.

It became apparent because of the structure and flexibility, that sharing the information while at the same time capturing it enables the customer to provide instant feedback. Furthermore, while refining what the salesperson was capturing, using the Clipboard allowed sellers to enhance the rapport already established.

Most salespeople adopt the broader structure of the FWIN Clipboard initially and go on to refine their approach over time. If you have an open mind, adopt what is working for you and come back later to implement some more until you have the instrument you need to D.R.I.V.E your success!

Why use the FWIN Clipboard in your customer situation?

We have found that one of the key ingredients to a successful sale is to build a shared understanding and a shared vision with the customer. On the Inside Track we demonstrate how asking the right questions and how interactive listening will help you to achieve a successful sale. Using the ubiquitous PowerPoint to display your information and a notebook to take notes could lead to a lack of engagement with the customer. If you genuinely want an interactive dialogue, use the FWIN Clipboard to illustrate your points, then take and share notes with your customer while in conversation. This will help in the following ways:

» Starting with a blank, white page lets your customer know that you are beginning your conversation without bias to a given solution and that you are prepared to listen and collaborate.

» Using the FWIN Clipboard helps you to stay flexible in your presentation, to jump from one subject to the other, while maintaining a clear structure as you progress towards the Ultimate Success Outcome.

» If you take notes of your customer's answers using the FWIN clipboard then sharing them as you write them down will enable you to validate the information and correct it on the spot.

» By utilizing the FWIN Clipboard, you put the information that the customer offers to you into a clear structure that in return might provide the customer with insight they did not have before.

» Using the FWIN Clipboard will help you overcome the potential challenge of having to ask too many questions.

For some salespeople, using an interactive way of presenting – one that involves asking questions and taking and sharing the answers from the customer is new. Our experience has consistently been that people who dare to use this new skill transform their client relationships and broaden their conversations regarding potential solutions. They significantly and consistently increase the size of the deals they close.

This chapter provides you with an introduction to the FWIN Clipboard and how to utilize it to your advantage in customer conversations.

The FWIN Clipboard is a vital tool that is used collaboratively with customers and colleagues to capture the core customer needs, challenges and potential solutions in one straightforward illustration. It can be used in two different ways:

1. **To Ask** - about the customer's situation and needs.

2. **To Ask and to Share** - your customer's and their industry's experiences.

The end results in both approaches will look very similar, even though how you use the Clipboard is quite different.

On the Inside Track, our emphasis is on active listening and providing the customer with insight from other customers in their industry. However, many salespeople do say that they sometimes feel a bit uneasy about repeatedly asking for the following reasons:

» Some salespeople may feel a bit anxious about asking a client about a subject they feel they should know more about themselves.

» Others say that some customers might feel interrogated or that perhaps as a salesperson you should already know the answers to all the questions you are asking.

This is why the clipboard is the perfect tool for the job. Imagine you have a slider on the bottom of the clipboard, one which you can move from 'Ask' to 'Tell' (we would prefer 'Share').

As your conversation with the customer progresses (using the D.R.I.V.E and B.R.A.K.E models you will learn later) you are able to gauge exactly how much you can ask (especially when you sense the customer is learning from their own answers) and how much you need to 'share' (when the customer does not know what is possible and what you have done for others in similar situations).

By capturing the customer's responses directly onto the FWIN Clipboard, you can refine and verify your understanding with them immediately and develop a shared understanding as you move along in the conversation. Importantly, when a customer is expecting advice from you, it is easier to show a Clipboard that you have already prepared in advance of your meeting. Spending time formulating and populating the FWIN Clipboard before a meeting means that during the meeting, you can focus totally on the customer, instead of thinking which PowerPoint slide you should be showing.

However, a word of caution - when using the FWIN Clipboard, you will need to remain flexible. If a customer cannot relate to something on the Clipboard that you prepared prior to the meeting, be ready to adjust it. Similarly, be prepared to adapt your approach to your customer. The more structure you have and the more prepared you are, the easier it becomes to adjust ad hoc.

The FWIN Clipboard is used in all three sales calls *(Discovery, Alignment and Closing)* to assist you in:

1. *Asking* the right questions
2. *Recording* the customer's answers as part of a conversation
3. *Presenting* your solution when the time is right
4. *Matching* your products to the customer's Ultimate Success Outcome is achieved through several interactions with them, in which you will *gather, exchange and present* information using the FWIN Clipboard.

The Clipboard is a vital, yet simple tool to Gather, Exchange and Present Inside Track information.

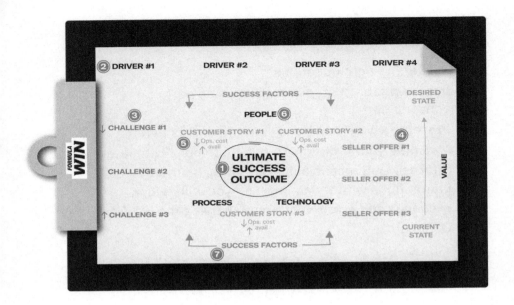

7 easy steps to using the clipboard

Starting at the center of the empty clipboard we begin by asking the customer what they are trying to achieve, that is to say what is their Ultimate Success Outcome. We then progress by asking the customer what drives their investments and about their current challenges (or roadblocks as we like to call them).

Here is a list of questions written in red that you can use immediately with very little adaptation needed. The sentence below each question explains what you are trying to find out:

1. **'What is it that you ultimately want to achieve?'**

    What is the Ultimate Success Outcome in the customer's industry?

2. **'What is forcing you to invest in new solutions?' or 'What is driving you?'**

    What drives the customer's investment to achieve the Ultimate Success Outcome?

3. **'What's stopping you from doing that?' or 'What is holding you back?'**

   What prevents the customer from achieving the Ultimate Success Outcome? In other words, what are the *Roadblocks* or *Challenges* they need to address?

4. **'How can we help you to achieve your ultimate success outcome?'**

   What can the customer do to address the drivers and overcome roadblocks? What *Value* are you able to offer with your products and services that will help the customer with these?

5. **'To show you a couple of relevant successes, here are some clients who are achieving their Ultimate Success Outcomes by partnering with us.'**

   Share stories that convey your message about how you helped others to be successful when facing similar situations.

6. **'How do we deliver the Ultimate Success Outcome that you are looking for?'**

   Explain how your People (and their capabilities), Processes and Technology help D.R.I.V.E your customer's success?

7. **'What Success Factors make us unique?'**

   How will the relationship between you and your customer be structured after they buy your product to D.R.I.V.E efficiencies and success?

Ideally, you come to the meeting with a blank page and fill it in throughout the conversation with your customer. To ensure your best outcome, it's advisable to prepare and to memorize a Clipboard that already contains deep insight into the industry and the customer's unique challenges and situation.

By working through each of the seven questions, a conversation ensues whereby both parties become aligned on the best outcome or solution and writing the answers on the Clipboard enables the customer to agree or to modify their answers on the spot.

1. What is the Ultimate Success Outcome in the customer's industry?

The center of the FWIN Clipboard is also called 'the goal'. Using it as a consultative selling tool, you come to the customer prepared with an Ultimate Success Outcome that works in their industry and is in tune with your products and services.

Here are two examples:

» From the IT support services industry, the Ultimate Success Outcome is very often to have 'Optimized Support'. This is defined as supporting the whole IT operations, including the data centers with the best quality resources within the available financial and personnel resources.

» From the logistics industry such a goal might be 'Better Fleet Productivity'. This means using the fleet of vehicles and associated staff in the most effective way.

» Including the Ultimate Success Outcome as part of the expectation in your introduction is always a good way to bridge the gap from your Introduction to Asking, Listening and Recording.

2. What Drives the customer's investment to achieve the Ultimate Success Outcome?

The answer to this question will allow you to group the answers under three to four main headings and these headings depict the areas which you know are key for this customer's specific role.

In the case of IT support services, they could be:

» Availability (of operational IT hardware and software)

» Cost (in common with most industries)

» Efficiency (how the IT department utilizes its key resources) and

» Flexibility (how quickly the department can respond to their customer demands)

For example, in Fleet Management, it could be: Operations, Efficiency, Empowerment or Cost.

Having the industry drivers prepared in advance demonstrates your insight and preparedness for the meeting.

Here are some industry examples:

Ultimate Success Outcome	Driver #1	Driver #2	Driver #3	Driver #4
IT department 'Optimized Support'	Availability of computing capacity	Cost reduction of IT department operations	Efficient use of all resources (including personnel)	Flexibility so that the IT department can perform
IT department 'Optimized Support'	Fleet maintenance	Efficiency in fuel and idle time	Technology	Optimization of time and job scheduling
Optimized Banking Operations	Digital transformation	Long term sustainable cost reduction	New legal structures	Governance and regulatory requirements

NB. It may happen that when a customer is asked about their Ultimate Success Outcome, they begin talking about their Drivers. This is fine. If they do, simply write down what they say under your driver headings for that industry. Then, circle back to say (in this case) 'Yes, we call these 'Drivers'. Explain that the reason you want to achieve such Drivers is to help them reach a higher-level goal that we call 'Optimized Support'.

3. What is preventing the customer from achieving their Ultimate Success Outcome, ie what are the Challenges they need to address?

Working *with* the customer to explore their challenges will help you to understand the environment in which they operate. Ideally, you will be aware of the general challenges in their wider industry before any meeting. Then during the consultation, you will capture the challenges described on the left-hand side of the FWIN Clipboard. We note the Challenges on the left depicting the existing situation. We write the challenges down in red, as this is a warning color and a situation we want to help move the customer away from.

Here are examples from different industries:

Ultimate Success Outcome	Challenge #1	Challenge #2	Challenge #3
IT department 'Optimized Support'	Skills and Training	Service Level Definitions inside the company	Increased complexity in their datacenter by having too many vendors and new technologies
Optimized Fleet 'Productivity'	Skilled and reliable staff	Vehicle utilization	Increased complexity from having more customers and more complicated routes to schedule.
Optimized Banking 'Operational Excellence'	Disintegration of the value chain (based on the possibility of sharing production and distribution processes between organizational units or external suppliers)	Maintaining economies of scale	Complexity: Increasing Complexity from the scope of activities, increased scale crossing countries, financial innovation and difficulties to evaluate financial risk in complex products.

4. How can the customer address the drivers and challenges and what Value can your products and services offer?

So far, you have predominantly asked questions and recorded the customer's responses. As we move into the Suggest phase, you will start to formulate a way to address the Drivers and overcome the Challenges that your customer faces. Here, you suggest a journey of added value and will move from basic value on the bottom to the optimum value at the top of the clipboard.

This journey is, in essence, how you can help your customer move from their current to the desired situation. Avoid using your company's jargon and acronyms and instead explain how you add value using the customer's language.

5. Can you describe who else is achieving the Ultimate Success Outcome through Stories?

During the Value journey, it is time to explain to the potential customer how other some of your other clients with similar needs are benefiting from using your products and services. You will do this using Customer Success Stories. There will be more on this in a later chapter.

6. *How can your People, Processes and Technology deliver the value?*

The credibility you deliver in this part of your suggestion focuses on your company's uniqueness and positions your oranization as a reliable and sustainable supplier of what you are selling.

How is your company able to deliver the value you explained earlier? We have found it works very well if you structure your response to this kind of question from the customer's perspective in three categories:

People: How are your people qualified in a unique way to deliver the Value?

Process: How do your unique processes provide the basis to deliver Value consistently?

Technology: What provides you with a leading edge?

How do you leverage the latest technology in the way you work?

By addressing all three areas above, you will demonstrate that your organization can provide a solution that adds real value to the buyer's operation in a reliable fashion that is well-designed and well-practiced.

7. *What Success Factors make you unique?*

While People, Process and Technology address the ability to deliver value, Success Factors focus on the partnership into which your customer enters with your company. Here, we communicate what makes your products and services unique and we show how they influence your future working relationship with your customer.

In summary

Gather, Exchange and Present information using the FWIN Clipboard

Linking your individual client's **Ultimate Success Outcome** to that of their company's strategy supports their internal decision-making power.

Drivers are the reasons why your customer must invest to achieve their Ultimate Success Outcome.

Challenges are the issues that prevent the customer from achieving their Ultimate Success Outcome.

Sharing your success stories using the clipboard is a powerful way to persuade your customer of the benefits in embarking on your suggested Value journey.

A balance of **Quantitative and Qualitative Value** are vital components shown to your customer on **their Clipboard**

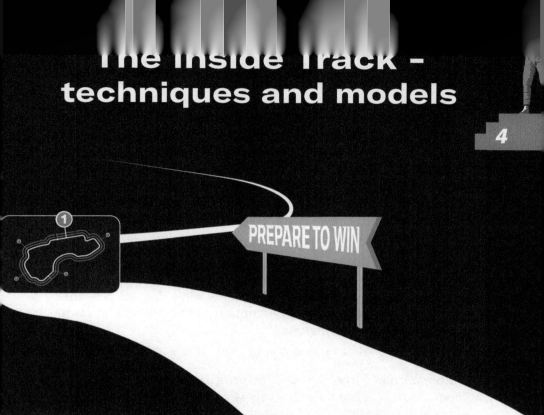

The inside Track – techniques and models

4

PREPARE TO WIN

"Most people have the will to win, few have the will to prepare to win."

~Bobby Knight

We would like to invite you to pause for a moment to reflect on 'What would happen if...' We hope this will help you recognize such potential crashes with customers that the following technique would help avoid.

'What would happen if'

» You visit a customer and when asked their CEO's name you don't know?

» You hadn't visited your customer's website or read their annual report?

» You confused a customer's flagship product line with one their competitors?

The benefit of being prepared is huge!

Let's consider for a moment the following:

- » How long does it take to get an appointment with a potential client?
- » How much preparation do you do prior to visiting a client? Does it vary?
- » How does that client know that you prepared in advance of the meeting?
- » Existing clients are also busy people and an appointment with a salesperson is for them a low priority. How can you prepare in such a way to change this perception and add value and unique insight to the conversation?
- » What do you do to prepare your own mental state?

A professional footballer trains five days a week to play one ninety-minute match. A Formula One racing car driver can work 12 hours a day at the racetrack and then go home to spend their evenings formulating a strategy to win the race.

Most sellers we meet agree that more time spent on preparation increases their win ratios and, as with any other discipline, the decision of how much time to spend on preparation rests entirely with you, the seller.

"When it comes to the more complex, higher-risk purchases, buyers want help cutting through the noise – 49% are overwhelmed with the amount of content out there, while 74% feel it's not personalised enough." [1] This suggests that preparation significantly increases the likelihood of winning.

With the right preparation, you will be able to find information about the client leadership's strategy and **Ultimate Success Outcome**. If you share this bigger picture with your individual customer, it will aid you in supporting their success in the internal decision making process. Sellers who only focus on the specific

---

1   Demand Gen Report (2016). 2016 Content Preferences Survey: B2B Buyers Value Content That Offers Data And Analysis. Retrieved 22 August 2021

request for a product very often miss this bigger picture and wider opportunities to engage with the client.

What to prepare?

Depending on the type of customer and the sort of industry you work in, the word 'preparation' has a variety of meanings. To a salesperson in a retail situation, it might simply be setting up the stall and keeping a tidy showroom. It could involve making sure the props are in the right places and that the showroom is clean and inviting. With a more complicated product or solution, preparation can become more challenging.

In our experience and since we mostly train sellers in a B2B evironment, the type of preparation you will need to do generally falls into gathering insight into the following areas:

Industry Knowledge

Buyers are 5 times more likely to buy from a B2B seller with industry insight. In a consultative sales scenario, the seller must be knowledgeable, interested and as passionate about the client's own business as you are about your own. A simple search on the internet enables you to find an abundance of information, such as annual reports, blogs, webinar presentations about company strategy and many news items. From this, you can build an accurate picture of the company and the prospective clients even before entering their office. Researching the person you are about to meet, from reading their social media profiles and articles they have published in newspapers, industry journals and magazines, helps you put the person and the business into context. It's also a perfect way to start a conversation and build rapport when you do meet.

Client Behavior Knowledge

Ideally, when an appointment is confirmed, you'll want to cultivate that initial rapport. We all have different ways in which we conduct ourselves with our clients. Some of us are more interested in the factual or numerical aspects of our products and solutions, whereas others may seek to avoid any conflict by having a 100% agreement on everything. Some salespeople appear more direct and forceful in their approach, while others prefer the recognition of being a creative and jovial partner. In all the above scenarios, a successful communicator will adapt their personal preferences to fit those of the client.

Product Knowledge

As well as being an expert in your products and services, you will need to read up on the latest competitive offerings and new/future identified needs. You'll also need to be aware of new technology in the market if this is your industry. This will help give you that competitive edge and make it easier for you to gain trust with well-informed potential clients. It will also help you to help your client make a more informed choice as they navigate 'similar offerings'.

Ultimate Success Outcome knowledge

Of executive decision makers in the IT industry, 74% stated that most sales professionals speak far too much about their products and not enough about the customer's Business Outcome. Knowing the difference between Product Outcomes and Success Outcomes is key to 'partnering' with customers, instead of 'selling' to them.

Finding the fit

More specific preparation will depend on which sales phase you are at, in the context of the overall interaction. The goal here is always that each person ends a call or a meeting having benefited.

Matching the products that you sell to the Ultimate Success Outcome is done through a number of client interactions. In these you will **gather, exchange and present** information using the FWIN clipboard as described in Chapter 3.

Ultimately, your customer's choice depends on the result of their interaction with you, the salesperson and it is how your preparation shines through into this customer experience which forms the foundation of your success.

Prepare for a Discovery Call

A Discovery Call is predominantly your chance to get to know what drives your customer's investments and the challenges they are facing. Here, it is useful to produce something that you can give back to the customer. This could be up-to-date industry information, or perhaps a recent white paper published by your company.

It's certainly worth planning how you will 'introduce' yourself, your company and your offering. Plan your questions for the discovery phase. How will you Discover – Refine – Impact – Verify and Expand on what the customer says? Also, what could you Suggest that you and the customer do after this call to progress things further?

The Discovery Call priority

You must leave this meeting knowing whether or not the client has a compelling need for which you can provide the solution. We call this The FWIN Compelling Action Reason (CAR). What is the reason that will force the customer to invest? For example, it could

NO CAR = NO SALE

be that the customer has expanded and cannot maintain delivery of their products without support from a company like yours.

Without a CAR, the customer doesn't have a reason to buy any of the products or services you have to offer.

Prepare for a Value Alignment call

To further add credibility and link your Value Alignment call with your previous meeting, you can inform the customer about the progress made since you last met. For example, you may consider preparing a report or sending an email in advance of the meeting.

If you are meeting with a person from your company whose support you will need to sell your offering to a customer, think about what's in it for them and appeal to this in any prior communications you send.

Prepare for a Closing Call

In a Value Alignment Call, you used open questions to demonstrate curiosity; however, during a Closing Call, you will be aiming to employ more closed questions to verify the information.

In this sales phase, it is more likely that you will be presenting your proposal to the customer with the expectation that they will sign a contract with you at the end. Therefore, it is crucial that you make this clear in your introduction. Remember, you will also need to prepare your Value message to the customer.

We highly recommend that you structure your presentation as outlined below.

The key is to open by attracting the audience's attention and hold it until the end, by which point it is the customer who has that all-important 'aha' moment. In their mind, this will connect your bold opening statement to the quantified Benefits you covered in point 4 below.

Although you might begin by preparing the client's situation and the quantified benefits of your product or service, it is important that your bold statement can only be verified by listening to your explanation of the solution (3) and the benefits (4). This way, you take the client on a journey and keep their attention for the entire presentation.

Here is our tried and tested sales presentation structure for your closing call:

1. A **Bold** statement (that gets attention)
2. Summary of your **client's** main **goals** ('we understand you')
3. Your **Solution**, described in the client's language (short and appropriate)
4. Quantified **Benefits** (time and money)
5. **Relevant** reference cases ('it already works')
6. **Why** choose you and your company? (Unique Value)
7. **Next** steps (to achieve their goals)

Many closing calls begin with 'the current situation'; essentially telling the client what they already know. Time and again, we have found this standard presentation style ineffective in keeping the senior management's attention. In their search for meaning – and due to their tendency to enjoy solving problems – it is better if you allow your audience the opportunity to add up the benefits for themselves. In essence, you provide the time and space for them to verify your Bold statement.

Next, we will explore a practical example of how you can present your solution in a Closing Call Scenario. We have indicated the reason why we include each element in brackets, followed by a summary description.

1. A Bold statement (gets attention)

This is a statement that promises to achieve the Ultimate Success Outcome and one which encourages your customer to want to know how this will be done. *"I am here today to present to you how our ACME Corporation will save XYZ Corp. **two million dollars** and increase your sales by 20% in the next 18 months."*

2. **The client's main goals ('we understand you and your solution')**

This is stated in words that you have heard the client use. These goals relate to the 'Drivers' and 'Challenges' on your clipboard (the important reasons that D.R.I.V.E the need for investment).

"You and your colleagues have told us how vital it is that you achieve the Ultimate Success Outcome so that your company can expand according to the corporate strategic plan agreed in March this year." (B2B research suggests the use of 'you-phrasing' can add urgency and make your prospect feel more personally responsible for solving the problem)[2].

3. **Your solution, described in the client's language (short and appropriate)**

To gain the optimum value we suggest that you invest in three areas:

» Solution A, to enable seamless management of your XYZ solutions.

» Solution B, to integrate your XYZ solutions and simplify usage.

» Solution C, make the information available to all who need access.

4. **The Quantitative (logical) value. Show the quantified benefits from this investment** (time and money):

» *"Solution A gives you a saving of 300,000 dollars."*

» *"Solution B increases your sales by 1,700,000 dollars."*

» *"Solution C allows you to speed up your goods to market which will increase customer satisfaction by 10% equating to a predicted increase in sales of one million dollars."*

Note how, as these quantities are revealed, they add up to those benefits stated in the opening Bold Statement, thereby allowing the client the opportunity to join the dots and be fully informed of the logic behind your explanation.

---

2   *Riesterer, T. (2021). 10 surprisingly effective sales techniques, backed by research. Retrieved 22 August 2021*

5. Share a Relevant Client Success Story ('it already works')

"As I shared with Ms. Smith, your sales director, our customer ABC Corp has already achieved a business outcome using a similar solution, tailored to their needs. We also helped another customer in the exact same industry do the same and finally we did... this..."

Salespeople need to embed long term memories by evoking memorable emotions. 'They need a reason to remember you'. Memories are reconstructed through narratives (they fill in the blanks with true or false information) and so by sharing a relevant client success story you will embed a positive emotion that resurfaces when they think of you.

6. Why choose you and your company? (unique value)

"Our company is unique in that we are the only provider of XYZ that can guarantee a 24-hour delivery time in all of the 52 states of the USA. We have worked in your industry for 30 years and continue to serve 50 other large companies in your field across 32 states."[3]

7. Next steps (to achieve client's goals)

"If you sign with us today, we will start here in San Francisco next week, followed by New York by the end of the month. Three weeks later we will complete the implementation in Atlanta."

Now that we have prepared to win for all three scenarios it is important to keep an open mind. As you conduct the calls with your customer, you will need to remain flexible and adjust, delete and add to your message and solution whenever needed – right up to the closing call.

Next is how you introduce yourself with impact.

---

3   Hart, R. (2017). *Customers need a reason to remember you.* Forrester. Retrieved 22 August 2021

'You never get a second chance to make a first impression'
~ **Will Rogers**

Introduce A.C.E

What would happen 'if'

» You introduce yourself with a cliché such as, 'Oh what a lovely office you have?'

» You cannot quickly convince your customer that your visit will be of value to them?

» Your customer doesn't know who you are or why you are there?

Your introduction opens the door!

It is essential that any introduction to a potential client be given your thorough attention.

» What are you going to say?

» How are you going to act with this particular client?

» How long will your introduction be?

» Do you introduce yourself every time you meet (the same) client? If so, in what way?

» How original or unique are you and how will you demonstrate this?

» How many other sellers before you entered the customer's office and commented on the décor or the view?

» How many spoke about the weather simply to break the ice?

AUTHENTICITY
CREDIBILITY
EXPECTATION

Prepare ⟩ Introduce ⟩ Ask, Listen, Record ⟩ Suggest ⟩ Confirm

Why use A.C.E?

The ACE introduction model provides you with an efficient and effective means of excelling at first impressions. These are the type of first impressions that enable you to start selling immediately.

Authenticity – How you act and what you say

'A' stands for Authenticity. What does that really mean? And how can you express it? You may say that it means 'to be yourself', 'to be honest' or 'to be sincere'. If we take the word sincere, the origin of which comes from the Latin 'Sine Cera' meaning 'without wax'. This was a message that ancient Roman pot makers would put on a sign outside their shops to show potential buyers that 'what you saw was what you got' and that they were not using wax to cover up any imperfections in the pots. Any heat applied to the pot would render it useless and the buyer would realize they had been tricked.

That is how you need to be with your customer - 'without wax'. It is clear to most customers that when your intention is aligned with their behavior, you are perceived as authentic and the chances of doing business with that person are elevated significantly.

The skill in showing authenticity is to strike a balance between mirroring your customer's behavior and values without omitting your own. For example if the customer expresses that they are a big tennis fan and you aren't, don't pretend that you are. It is just as authentic to acknowledge their love for the game and say that you have tried it and that you decided to stick to football instead.

In this way you are mirroring the common topic of sport that you both appreciate, while remaining authentic in your views.

How you act and what you say tells the client a lot about your attitude and whether you are behaving authentically or not. Are you optimistic and not arrogant? Are you respectful and not overly flattering?

Since most people nowadays appear to rely more on visual representation, what we wear and how we act in those first seconds contribute immensely to how we are seen.

The way that you greet your future or existing client will ensure that your authenticity shines through in your body language, your words and your energy. Sincerity and energy are the keys to attitude.

A word on cultural differences. While the nature of doing business is becoming increasingly relaxed, particularly in the West, in many countries professional titles are still appreciated. If in doubt, ensure you check beforehand so that you act in respectful accordance with your clients' culture.

Credibility – Why are YOU the right person to speak to?

Clients are busy people - why they should be spending a portion of their precious time speaking to you?

Simply explaining to the client an aspect of your previous industry experience or a little about a relevant qualification is an excellent way of putting their mind at rest. It is the opportunity to demonstrate that you are *the* partner needed to solve their challenge or help them fulfill their business needs.

This is also the opportunity to offer a case study to illustrate a successful project you were responsible for successfully delivering. Of course, it helps if this project is industry-specific and directly relevant.

Remember, influencing the customer's perception of your credibility will earn you the right to ask vital questions. This is precisely the reason that establishing your credibility in the introduction phase is imperative.

Afraid to 'blow your own trumpet'?

If you are uncomfortable with 'telling' your client about yourself, you might want to let the client join the dots themselves. For example, you can 'show' rather than 'tell' by saying something like: 'Your situation reminds me so much of a client that I helped a couple of years ago when this type of solution came on the market.' This sentence allows your client to recognize your experience and expertise with the solution that you are introducing.

Another way to establish credibility is to prepare something of interest and benefit to the potential client. If this is the first meeting, you will have read about the company on the Internet or spoken to a colleague or friend who has connections with the business to gain further insight.

We have met many sellers who say they 'always' do this. However, when we ask if they specifically told the client about the information they had found during their preparation in a follow-up coaching session after the client meeting, 90% say that they did not mention it. They often say that they do mention it if it comes up in conversation. In our opinion, this is like holding a great hand in a card game and only using it if the other player asks you to play it. Why wait to be asked?

By explaining your efforts, you are showing that you genuinely care and that you are serious about helping your client. Meaning that even if your competitor did the same amount of research (or more!) and does not tell the customer, you still retain the advantage.

This is also the opportunity to offer a case study to illustrate a successful project you were responsible for successfully delivering. Of course, it helps if this project is industry-specific and directly relevant.

Remember, influencing the customer's perception of your credibility will earn you the right to ask vital questions. This is precisely the reason that establishing your credibility in the introduction phase is imperative.

Expectation - why you are here today?

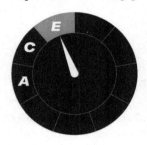

There must be a clear explanation of why you are there and the expected outcome of the meeting. This is the perfect moment to clarify the reason for the meeting and to set an agenda. Confirming the client's available time, and asking what their additional expectations are, shows respect for them and their schedule.

A.C.E example:

Good morning Mrs Schmidt, thank you for inviting me. My name is Jonathon Jones. I am the account manager for ACME. I've been working in the IT sector for more than 25 years and in the IT security business for more than 10 years, doing everything from systems engineering to operations before moving to sales.

I'd like to have a dialogue today to look at how you can transform your IT security to Enable a Secure Business and save up to 30% of your cost. We see opportunities for our clients to weave a Security Fabric optimized for cost, risk and business support. I want to share some of the drivers and challenges we see. We have been in the security business for over 20 years, so we can share some of what we have experienced during this time. Most importantly, I am interested in the issues from your perspective and your priorities.

Is there anything else you would like to add? You said in your email that you have a maximum of 45 minutes. Is that right?

An A.C.E Introduction for every client meeting

It is easy to see that for a first meeting, the three A.C.E steps are essential to gain enough rapport to move onto the dialogue that follows. What about when you meet a client for a second, third or even fourth time?

AUTHENTICITY
CREDIBILITY
EXPECTATION

Here are some examples of A.C.E introductions made at various stages on the sales circuit:

First meeting

Good afternoon Mr Sinclair, my name is John Jones. You have shown interest in our ABC product and I'm here today to show you how you can save up to 30% of the cost you have today. I've worked in this industry for 20 years; perhaps you remember the XYZ project?

Yes, that was quite an interesting one; I was responsible for supplying all of the parts on time and looking after the project management that was vital to the timely completion. Before I came here today, I took the initiative of reading about your current project on your website and I saw that you are looking for the ABC solution. I would like to suggest that we use the following agenda...

Follow-up meeting

Hello Mr Sinclair. Thank you for agreeing to this meeting at such short notice. I realize your urgent need to press on with the project, so I have brought you the printed drawings which I sent to you yesterday by email. I have also invited Mr Singh, our valve expert, to help with any of the more technical queries you might have. The great news is that I can see a clear path to the 30% cost saving mentioned in the earlier meetings, so we are on track. Do you have any questions or any comments before continuing the discussion around the ACME pressure value issue?

Pre-proposal meeting

Good morning, Jim. Nice to see you again, how was your skiing trip last week? As we agreed last time, I've done some further preparation and have brought you the specifications that I agreed with your Quality Assurance department yesterday. Your Quality Assurance team have confirmed the potential savings and were very positive. Before I present our solution, do you have any questions or comments that need to be added to the agenda today?

Negotiate and close meeting

Good afternoon ladies and gentlemen. For those who I have not yet had the pleasure of meeting, my name is John Williams. I am responsible for providing high-value solutions to ACME's most valued customers. Even after 20 years with ACME I am still very excited to engage in new projects such as yours. I have been working closely with Mr Sinclair over the last week to understand your exact needs. I can now match them with the optimum/ideal solution presented last week. In my initial meeting, I mentioned the possibility of saving up to 30% of your current cost. Subsequent sessions confirmed that we will be able to achieve 28% and simultaneously enable you to accelerate your innovation cycle by 23%. I'm here today to answer any further questions that will allow you to make your final decision.

 **Inside Track - A.C.E**

Below, we would like you to now write your own A.C.E introduction in preparation for your next client visit. This can be for a new customer, or for one you have known for a longer period. Once you have written it down, read it back to yourself aloud. How does it sound? Is it appropriate? Feel free to fine-tune it until you are ready to use it in a real-life scenario. Finally practice by reading it to your co-driver.

Notes:

Ask, Listen, Record

What would happen if:

» You left the client without asking them about their needs?

» You didn't learn the potential impact that your service could have on your client's business?

» You didn't remember any of the information given to you by the client?

Asking, Listening and remembering are vital!

After establishing rapport and aligning with your client on the expectations for this meeting, you are now ready to ask some questions. Before we do this, let us take a moment to think about how we can listen to and record those answers.

Telling or selling?

To achieve a deep understanding of your client, it will be necessary to ask many questions. Ideally, these questions will be balanced with information and insight that you can provide based on your industry knowledge and experience. In cases when a client asks to be told about your products and services, it is of course fine to elaborate briefly. However, if you want to close the deal, we recommend that you spend a considerable amount of time asking questions to ensure a full understanding of your clients situation.

The **Ask, Listen and Record** stage of the model is arguably the most important aspect of this book.

Interactive Listening – The B.R.A.K.E model

This chapter shows you how to listen effectively and how to gather the vital information needed to progress with or disengage from a potential opportunity.

As a salesperson, you probably listen to the client for two main reasons:

1. To understand their needs, so that you can provide best value;
2. To build rapport.

Remember, to have an answer worth listening to, you need to ask great questions!

» How does the customer know you are listening?
» How do you know if someone is listening to you?
» How do you detect if someone is listening because they genuinely want to help you?
» What makes you feel that someone is only listening to that which could benefit them?
» Why do we sometimes suffer from selective hearing?

Your answers to these questions are the basis upon which to develop the skills needed to build trust with a client.

Selective hearing is a barrier to true listening

There is a large research base into selective hearing regarding why and how our brains have evolved this way.[1]

When recently working with a group of salespeople, we stopped the session and announced a single word, completely out of context. That word was 'coffee'. Immediately half of the group rose to their feet. Three of them had already made it to the espresso machine before we could stop them to talk about selective hearing and selective interpretation. We hadn't

---

1   Coch, D., Sanders, L. D. and Neville, H. J. (2005). An event-related potential study of selective auditory attention in children and adults. J. Cogn. Neurosci. 17, 605–622

announced an actual coffee break, however those members of the group who were up on their feet had heard what they wanted to hear and acted accordingly.

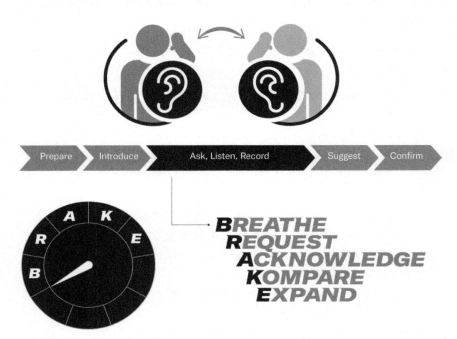

Imagine the scene. You are driving along in an open top convertible across the Swiss Alps and you faintly hear your mobile ring. You answer via your speakerphone, however the noise of the wind is making it impossible to hear the other person. Your natural reaction is to slow down, so you literally put your foot on the brake.

Just as braking in a car reduces the outside noise, 'braking' in a client meeting gives both parties space to breathe and focus on the conversation.

B.R.A.K.E stands for:

*B*reathe,
*R*equest, Record and Respond,
*A*cknowledge and Ask,
'*K*ompare' and
E for Expand

Let's look at B.R.A.K.E in a little more detail:

Breathe. Without drawing undue attention to yourself, take one or two conscious breaths. You will experience the immediate calming effect this has on your whole physiology and way of being. When you take a deep breath in, you cannot talk but you are able to listen instead.

Request. Ask if it's OK to take some notes. This shows that you are actively listening and that what the client is saying is important enough to capture.

Record (with a pen and paper). Knowing that you are recording what they say, your client will subconsciously begin to describe their challenges and current situation with much greater clarity. This, in turn, means that you will have the chance to get the best possible insight into how you can help. Ideally, you will record this on the FWIN Clipboard and share it with the customer along the way. By doing so, you are also building shared understanding and buy-in and, if the customer does not object to what you write, they implicitly agree.

Respond. Offering physical cues like nodding and responding to what the customer says and with affirmative statements such as 'OK', 'I see' or 'interesting', are all ways to show that you are actively listening to what they have to say.

Acknowledge. Your physical and verbal responses demonstrate that you hear what your customer is saying and understand their point of view. Asking relevant, qualifying questions while taking notes is vital, because it maintains rapport and also because this helps you discover as much as you can about the customer's experience, needs and wishes.

Kompare (written with a K to make the acronym work!). This is when you compare what the customer is saying to what he or she said earlier in your conversation, or compared to what they may have told you last time you spoke. Needs, wishes and experiences evolve, so Kompare can help you establish if your current understanding is right. By doing this, you confirm that you were listening for information and also genuinely curious and keen to get things right.

*E*xpand. A customer will often discover new needs or wishes simply by having you as a sounding board. Asking, 'Is there anything else?' – or words to that effect – will open up the dialogue for more information to come. The less you say, the more you will both learn about the unique world of this specific customer.

Listen for 'Signals'

Buddhist monks are said to believe that it is the gaps between the notes that make the music. Similarly, we believe that the seemingly inconsequential comments a client shares about their situation hold vital significance. If you listen to a conversation between two people who have rapport, you often find apparently unimportant comments are added which are never probed.

These comments are signals and when you are listening with intense focus, you hear them. Viewed in this context, signals are in fact invitations for you to explore your client's subconscious concerns that even they may not yet be aware of. From this perspective, we like to view signals as subconscious indicators that a client might need further help with something that isn't yet on the agenda.

Salespeople who work at the level of the subconscious mind are certain to gain the Inside Track.

So, to recap. What can, on the surface appear to be a seemingly unimportant comment can often lead to something significant, even crucial if you hear and then question it:

Customer: *"And that would depend on the July results."*

Salesperson: *"You mentioned the results in July. Why are they important?"*

The Questions to D.R.I.V.E the conversation

"If you want to listen to an interesting conversation, you must ask the right questions" Beat Erb

In this chapter, we elaborate on the types of questions which are most effective in gathering the information we need, while at the same time enabling us to maintain and build the relationship.

Asking Questions

A concern we hear repeatedly from sales managers is that their salespeople do not ask clients 'the right questions'.

When we ask customers what the 'right' questions are, we hear 'questions which are neither leading nor manipulative toward making a sale'. How do we ask questions which are not manipulative or leading?

Salespeople want to look competent in front of their customers and they think it is important to 'have all the answers'. We believe that this is only true to some extent.

A salesperson should have good knowledge of their products and services. Ideally, they will have a decent amount of industry experience and experience selling to other clients with similar challenges.

A salesperson also needs to understand a customer's challenges and foresee challenges they don't yet know about. Customers might not be able or willing to share this level of information. Therefore, getting the level of detail you need requires you to ask a lot of questions which can become uneasy for the customer. In our experience, there are a few strategies that can help:

» Take notes of the questions using the FWIN clipboard and share them with your customer as you go along. The structure of the FWIN Clipboard helps you and the customer to put the answers into perspective.

» When you share the customer's answers on the FWIN clipboard, they can validate and correct them on the spot.

» By having the FWIN Clipboard, you put the information the customer provides you with into a clear structure that in turn might give the customer insight they did not have before.

In essence, using the FWIN Clipboard will help you to overcome the potential challenge of seeming to have to ask a lot of questions.

Question Types

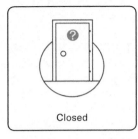
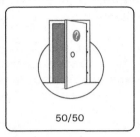
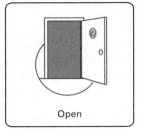

Closed   50/50   Open

We will explore three types of questions in this chapter: Open, Closed and 50/50.

A Closed Question can only be answered by a yes or a no. These types of questions are predominantly used to clarify or verify understanding, e.g. 'If I understand you correctly, this would be a game-changer for you and your company - is that right?'

Whereas they are a useful technique to clarify information, they do however create a long and tedious journey towards eliciting big picture and rapport building information.

The type of question often 'overused' by salespeople simply trying to extract information from customers is *the 50/50 type question*. Such questions often elicit a short, one-word answer by utilizing words such as when, how and how much. For example:

» When will you start?
» How much is that?
» How many?

Although these questions are extremely important and must be used to obtain specific information, they must be used with care as their overuse can give the recipient the feeling that they are being interrogated.

A Sales Call is a CONVERSATION

NOT AN INTERROGATION

An Open Question is defined as a question that elicits a longer and more revealing answer. Open questions usually start with 'why', 'how' or 'what do you think'. Although 'why' can be a good option, do be careful using it in response to a negative statement as it can become personal or politically charged. For example, 'I think your product is too expensive!', 'Why?' (asking 'why' can appear defensive whereas 'what makes you say that' works fine).

Some useful examples might be:

- » What challenges are you facing in the marketplace?
- » When would you need the new system to make the biggest impact?
- » Where can this help you to achieve your Ultimate Success Outcome?
- » Who is part of the decision-making process?
- » How might this change the way you work?
- » How much more can you produce once the new system is in place?
- » Why is this important to you?

Open Questions are best utilized when looking to explore and get information from your customer. Be ready to note down their answers on your FWIN Clipboard.

Although it may be true that Open Questions offer more information than closed ones, once you have developed rapport, your client will begin to answer even Closed Questions with a detailed explanation. Your genuine curiosity and interest in understanding another person will D.R.I.V.E your questions towards mutual success. Ultimately, a balance of all three types of questions will give you the range of information that you need to help your client buy your solution.

Asking the right questions might take some practice. However, we believe that it is more important for the conversation to flow naturally than to get every question perfect and so it's worth being flexible with your approach.

Will you take notes?

We have already explored how taking notes shows you are listening with active interest and respect. Clients tend to think carefully about the details they give you and it is vital that you record this key information, especially numbers, time-frames and budgets, etc. This data can prompt further questioning and, if needed, can also buy you time to think.

Asking your client if it is OK to take notes draws attention to your serious intent to listen. It also allows you to introduce the FWIN Clipboard introduced in chapter 3.

There are several reasons to collaborate with your customer on note-taking. The FWIN Clipboard keeps the conversation centred on the Ultimate Success Outcome and prevents you from drifting too far into other subjects. If you share your notes as you go along, the customer might help you put their answers into perspective. Used correctly in this context, the Clipboard (or Flipchart or Whiteboard) enables you to retain a structure in your dialogue with your customer and contain the conversation within a productive parameter.

Seeing you write a statistic or, indeed, any other aspect of your conversation can trigger your customer into providing even more information. Here, you can also provide any relevant industry insight, which may provoke further ideas.

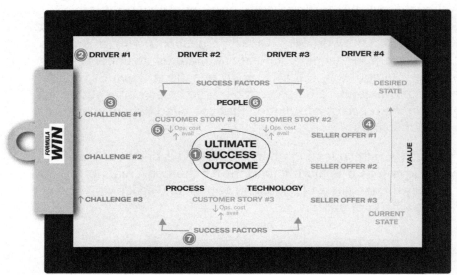

In our experience, customers will want a copy of the clipboard, because they see new insights emerging and can imagine themselves needing to refer to them in the future.

Making questions more comfortable

Also known as: Prefacing Questions, or in other words, 'why am I asking?'

In our sales training workshops, we notice that an obstacle to asking *the right question* is when a salesperson feels uncomfortable asking probing questions. If the salesperson is uncomfortable, this will undoubtedly put the customer on edge and we want to avoid this.

In our experience, a proven way to alleviate discomfort when asking probing questions is to put the questions into context for your client. You can do this by letting the customer know why you are asking them and then simply ask away. The following examples show you what we mean. Bear in mind as you read, that the text in bold can help you come up with your own questions.

Examples:

To get the design right, I need to ask you some questions about the bigger picture of your operation. How exactly are your products produced from start to finish?

So that we can work on a solution that will match your needs, I would need to know your expected budget for the project.

To make the best use of your time today, I would like to get a bigger picture regarding your ABC project's main issues. Therefore, I'd like to ask you why you want to...

So as not to 'bark up the wrong tree' it's beneficial for me to know the people involved in the various parts of the project and their roles.

Next, let's take a closer look at the D.R.I.V.E model.

What would happen if'

» You only asked questions that gave the customer a feeling of being interrogated?

» You didn't find out why the customer was looking for a new product or service?

» You didn't verify the clients wishes before leaving?

The questions you ask can build or ruin a client/seller relationship!

We have designed the D.R.I.V.E model to help you ask the right type of question to gather information, understand the customer's potential needs and challenges and develop solutions to achieve the Ultimate Success Outcome. Notice that in the picture, three phases of D.R.I.V.E are there to narrow down and refine, whereas two of them will then help you return to a specific subject.

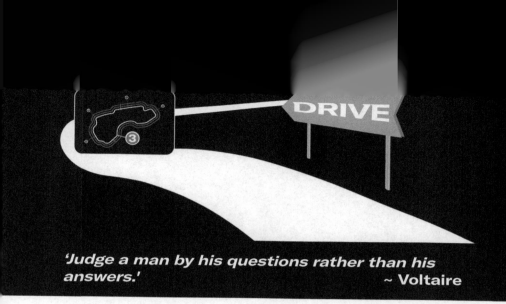

'Judge a man by his questions rather than his answers.'
~ **Voltaire**

Structured Questioning - The D.R.I.V.E model

D.R.I.V.E helps you to:

» **Structure** both you and your client's conversation.

» Inspire **Confidence** in your ability to understand your customers situation.

» **Collaborate** to garner insight with your customer.

» Demonstrate your industry **Knowledge**.

» Convince your client of your **Competence**.

» Be in **Control** of the meeting.

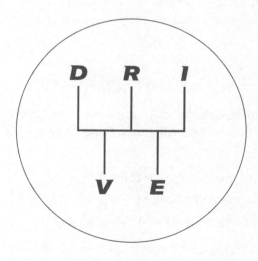

The D.R.I.V.E model intuitively works with the natural flow of conversation and consists of various types of questions that you can use to gather information from your client.

These conversations often begin with 'big-picture' style **D**iscovery questions, followed by asking for more **R**efined detail. Information is then **V**erified to confirm your understanding. In such a dialogue, one person might ask a 'what if' question, which influences the customer to think about their desired Ultimate Success Outcome. They may also consider the **I**mpact of making a decision or taking no decision. Such dialogues often branch off into talking about other related topics that are **E**xpanded upon by asking more open questions.

Discover, Refine and Impact are often used to narrow down a conversation, while Verify and Expand open it up again. In this context, Expanding enables you to widen the focus on a more specific topic.

Discover - building the bigger picture

Discover-type questions are predominantly open questions. In the Discover phase, you will be seeking answers for the following questions:

» What brings the client here today?
» What is the main challenge for the client?
» What is the bigger picture in the business?

Let us look at the specific challenges in the Discover phase.

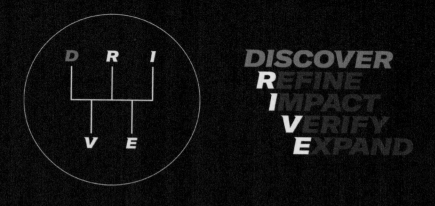

The Discover Challenge

As we have already established earlier in this chapter, it is useful in making questions more comfortable if you explicitly explain to the customer why Discover questions need to be asked. An example of how you might do this would be:

*"**To make the best use of your time** I'd like to take a step back and discover the bigger picture behind the challenges you are facing. I am going to use a structure that will help us focus and share my notes with you as the bigger picture emerges. Is that OK with you?"*

We know that by using the structure of the FWIN Clipboard and sharing the answers back to the customer as you move along, a bigger picture of their challenges is emerges. During the conversation, the customer will open up and may provide even more information.

If this is not clearly communicated early in the dialogue, the client could become uncomfortable with the conversation.

Discover questions show the client that you are truly interested in learning about their business and we have already explored when to use them and when they work best. To build on this, here are some examples you could use in the **Discover** phase of the conversation:

» What is your opinion of...?
» Why do you think that?*
» How is the market changing?

» What do you think will happen?

» Why does that not sound right?

» What in your opinion does the best solution look like?

» What makes you say that?

» How do you feel about that?*

» What do you think about such solutions?*

Asking what a client thinks and feels is a powerful way to connect with their emotions and in our experience, is a great way to get to know your client on a more personal level.

Sharing your Discoveries using the FWIN Clipboard gives you more time to take notes and provides a structure to help you think of the next question. Used in conjunction with the FWIN Clipboard, the following questions can help you to uncover your customer's Ultimate Success Outcome:

» What do you want to achieve? (Where you begin to discover the Ultimate Success Outcome)

» Why is this important for you and your company? (Find out the drivers of investment)

» What is holding you back? (Uncover the challenges your customer is facing)

 **Discover**

Now it's your turn. Think of more Discover-type questions that you can imagine asking your clients. Read them out loud and imagine how you would answer if you were in the customer's shoes.

Notes:

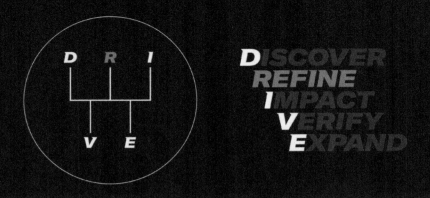

Refine - asking for details

After building the bigger picture of a situation, it is natural in any conversation to ask additional questions that establish the details needed to understand the customer's answers better and more specific.

To achieve this, we recommend you ask 50/50 Questions which demand a shorter answer during the Refine phase of the conversation. That will help you to convert the bigger picture into more specific needs. Possible questions are often around dates, time schedules, budgets etc. and enable you to:

» Ask for more detail about the current situation.
» Understand what is behind the needs and the wants of the client.
» Get a better picture of the numbers in terms of people, time and money.

The Refine challenge

Questions to Refine, when asked too early and too often in a sales conversation, can make the client feel somewhat suspicious. In a rapid-fire scenario, the client might feel more like they are in an interrogation than a conversation! If used in this way, they could also be perceived as coming from a place of self-interest i.e., only seeking information that will benefit your ability to close a deal. During Refine, the 50/50 questions listed below will ordinarily draw a response of a single word or number:

» How much?

» How many?

» When is your deadline?

» How many do you need?

» Which color would suit you?

» How long have you used this system?

» What is your budget?

As we have already established, prefacing your questions helps to prepare the way for **R**efining to be welcomed as part of the conversation. Sharing the answers with your customer on the FWIN Clipboard as you ask them will help to keep them engaged.

Our experience shows that your customer will most likely answer **R**efine questions more openly when they are asked in conjunction with D.R.I.V.E This is where your efforts reach fruition: your competition is much less likely to receive the same level of detail and will therefore have challenges in offering the same value to the customer.

Used in conjunction with the FWIN clipboard, the following examples can help you to identify your customer's key Drivers:

» How many outages did you experience last year?

» By when do you need to finish the project?

» Where is your biggest market?

 **Refine**

Now, think of some more Refine style questions you could ask your client. Read them out loud and reflect on about how you might answer if you were the customer. Doing so will help you to get into your customer's shoes and feel what it might be like to be asked those questions.

Notes:

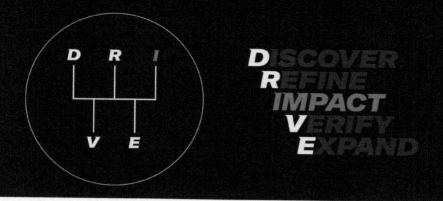

Impact - influencing the Customer

While building trust, a good salesperson cultivates their client's Compelling Action Reason. A need, of course, that can be solved by investing in their product or service.

Impact questions encourage the client to think deeply about the possible impacts, both positive and negative, on their business that relate to this investment. While many salespersons would prefer to paint a rosy, post-sale picture in the customer's mind, very often clients are more influenced by the potential negative impact of making the wrong decision. It's therefore crucial for you to ask the right questions and facilitate a conversation around this confidently. What's more, as client:seller rapport plays such an important role in the client's propensity to answer questions, it is vital to know when and how to deliver an Impact question.

Don't worry, we are going to show you precisely how to do this.

Why ask Impact questions?

Impact questions will help you discover what your customer values about your product or service. You can use them to discover both quantitative value (remember, this is value that you can calculate, for example, the cost of a service outage) and qualitative value (for example, improved employee's satisfaction due to a new system).

An Impact question is also the perfect way to remove the price objection.

Imagine for a moment that you are with a customer and you ask the following question:

Salesperson: *'What do I need to win this business?'*

Now, out of all of the possible ways the conversation may flow from this point, it is our experience that the customer is most likely (by which we mean 'almost certain') to say, *'lower your price'.*

The question sounds desperate and what is worse is that the customer has an automatic opportunity to take control and focus on a price-led discussion.

Instead, asking an Impact question will take their mind away from price, towards thinking about the possible impact on their business and ultimately, in favor of your solution:

» How much productivity was lost last year due to employees' dissatisfaction with the current system?

» Who is affected by the current situation?

» Why is it important to solve the problem?

» How will this solution improve your life?

Negative Impact questions are best asked when you have already established rapport with your customer. If you ask a Negative Impact question prior this, you run the risk of being perceived to be aggressively trying to close the deal.

The Impact Challenge

A genuine and effective Impact question asked by a seller who truly cares about the client's results and who the client justifiably trusts, comes from a place of customer interest.

Here are some generic Impact questions:

» How will on-time delivery benefit you personally?

» What will be the implications if the project is delayed?

» Have you seen the results of the XYZ company's attempt to save on lower quality materials?

» Other than price, what else is important here to make your project a success?

» How do you imagine your project management working with more than ten separate suppliers?

» How do you imagine your guests will react to this contemporary Italian interior design?

Bringing the tools together

Let us bring together the elements of what you are learning here with the FWIN Clipboard.

Impact questions are instrumental when used in conjunction with the FWIN Clipboard. They first help identify your customer's challenges and establish what is holding the customer back from achieving their goal.

For the best impact, once you ask a question, share your customer's answer on the FWIN Clipboard. Remember, by doing this, you create a situation whereby the customer either has to agree with you or provide you with more information until the statement is 100% correct. This will help you build a shared vision of their challenges and deepen your rapport.

The following examples can help you to identify your customer's Challenges:

» What is stopping you achieving your goal?
» Which areas of the company hinder your progress?
» What are your biggest challenges?

 **Impact**

Think of three more Impact questions you could ask a customer. Read them out loud and think about how you would answer if you were the customer.

Notes:

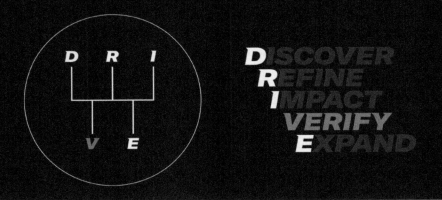

Verify - checking what you know is correct

Verify questions are typically closed questions, which require a simple 'yes' or 'no' answer.

After an information gathering session with a client, you might spend hours preparing a proposal upon which the chances of winning the deal depends. Will you rely on memory, or would it be better to clarify your understanding with the client before leaving?

Verify questions demonstrate to your client that you were listening and interested. The client is also reassured that everything they explained was received and will be acted upon.

Too many mistakes at this stage will give the impression that you have not listened, which can lead to a loss of trust. Verifying questions must be asked sparingly to avoid sounding like a checklist. It is better to choose the most critical points to summarize and capture the client's most influential needs.

A natural way to Verify is using the FWIN Clipboard. By writing the answers down and sharing them as you write them, you can verify with the customer as well as summarize the information you got from Discover, Refine and Impact questions.

You can show the client what they have already verified about their business and will be able to move across the FWIN Clipboard to your suggested next steps.

Here are some example Verify questions:

» You said that you need to raise production by 13%, is that right?
» Do you need all goods delivered to the same address?

» Did you say that the impact of a late delivery could cause significant delays and losses of 28%?

» So, you would like to have a single supplier if possible, to reduce risk?

Bonus benefit:

The moment of Verification is also the chance to upsell (a typical hamburger seller technique, 'Supersize' comes to mind). In the case of a more complex opportunity, you can take this opportunity to ask any questions you may have forgotten the first time around!

 **Verify**

Which Verify questions could you ask a customer? Write them below and then read out loud. Consider how you would answer them if you were the customer.

Notes:

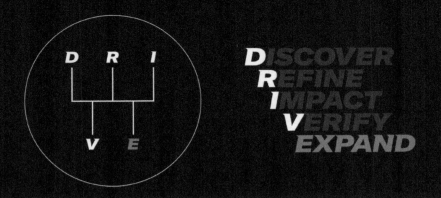

Expand - searching for more opportunities

During a client conversation, a salesperson often discovers signals that could lead to other needs being identified that were not mentioned before, or possibly even thought of by the customer during the conversation.

Expanding on these signals may lead to further opportunities and it's a natural way to pick up on something the client said earlier in conversation. In addition there may be opportunities to refer to something which you have noticed in the client's market.

Taking note of the signals on the FWIN Clipboard makes this an easier task. If focusing on signals hinders the current conversation's natural flow, you could choose to place them on a 'parking lot' on the FWIN Clipboard to come back to later in the conversation.

The Expand part of the conversation is an opportunity to find out more about other projects, or another need that might exist for the client.

The Expand challenge:

Expand questions are useful in your first – or possibly second – meeting with your customer. When you are closing a deal or want the client to focus on your solution, expanding the conversation again might cause an unnecessary distraction and delay the closing of the contract. In this scenario, you might have to come back to the subject once the deal is closed and start your next conversation.

Here are some Expand questions as an example:

» You mentioned that the project would also need some consultancy work. What do you mean by that?

» In which other countries do you intend to expand your activities?

» Since we are talking about fitting these kitchens in new houses, what will you be doing about the bathrooms and the home offices?

Bonus benefit:

Expand questions also allow you to cross-sell and offer leads to colleagues in other parts of your organization (for example, professional services). Expanding also helps with rapport building. It shows you were genuinely listening and interested in what the customer said and are willing to assist beyond your initial offering. Crucially, it demonstrates you are prepared to help even when there is no direct benefit to you.

 *Expand*

Where could you use an Expand question with your customers? Within this, think of areas where you could cross-sell. It is also worth considering the market that you are working in and give some thought to what other customers are doing right now. Formulate questions that you could ask your customer. Read them out loud and think about how you would answer them if you were in the customer's shoes.

Notes:

SPARK: A reminder to use D.R.I.V.E

When you are next at a client visit, before getting out of your car, glance down at the gear-shift as you turn off your engine. This visual Spark will remind you of the D.R.I.V.E methodology we introduced earlier.

Remember: Sparks are those cues we can use in our physical environment that remind us to act, to think differently or to behave in a certain way with a customer.

It is useful to note:

» To D.R.I.V.E successfully, you will need to utilize all available gears during the conversation

» Avoid staying in one gear for too long

» To gain trust and rapport and to learn about the client and their drivers and challenges, stay in Discover for a while to find out how you can add value

» Going immediately into Refine might lead to a one-sided search for information and break your rapport

» You do not have to stick to the D.R.I.V.E steps in the order they are written. Just like driving a car we move up and down the gears as necessary.

» You must remember to ask (good) Impact questions. Without any perceived impact the client does not have a good enough reason to invest. This impact will also influence the judgment to invest now rather than later.

Using the FWIN Clipboard gives you a structure that will keep you on The Inside Track. Use it in the Discover phase to structure the conversation and cover the areas needed. Note the customer's responses and information directly on the FWIN Clipboard to Refine and Verify information with the customer in the moment. Ask Impact questions to find the quantitative and qualitative value your solution brings to the table. Remember to Expand on subjects that in turn expand your solution or help you to cross-sell within your organization.

Suggest

What would happen if ...

» You left your customer not knowing what they should do next?

» You didn't show your customer the value of your offering compared to your competitor's?

» You push so hard that you try to close the deal before suggesting something that reassures your customer?

To Suggest is to Influence

Your main goal in the Suggest chevron is to persuade your customer to take the next step with you on a shared journey towards their Ultimate Success Outcome (U.S.O.) and to close the sale.

The actual suggestion you make to your client depends upon the conclusions you have reached during your meeting(s) and upon which Sales Phase you and your client are currently in.

The biggest challenge we face in this stage of The Inside Track is holding back from pushing the customer into buying when they are not yet ready. Before attempting to propose a solution, be sure that the customer is convinced that you have fully understood the Drivers and Challenges that their company is facing.

At the same time, we want to leave the customer knowing of and interested in, the value that we have to offer.

Prepare > Introduce > Ask, Listen, Record > Suggest > Confirm

Getting this balance right is key to moving the sale closer toward the close. Therefore, it is essential that you manage this element of the conversation skillfully. You are aiming to ensure that the customer remembers something about the 'Value' you can provide, even if no product name is mentioned.

'Value' - the key to strategic advantage!

A strong focus on value can bring about real strategic advantage. Consumer psychology theory and research consistently support the stance that perceptions around value are vital in sales conversations and strategy, even more so than price. These are commonly referred to as 'customer-perceived value' which is the customer's belief that a product or service has the ability to meet their needs or expectations. Simply put, to maintain a high level of customer perceived value, a product must provide physical, logical, or emotional benefit for the customer.

But recent Gartner research also emphasizes the importance of value in service interactions. This research has identified *'a reliable way for customer service to increase customer loyalty and decrease disloyalty'.*

They call this approach 'Value Enhancement'—boosting the value customers perceive in the actual product or service they've purchased. In driving that kind of outcome, Value Enhancement ultimately expands the customer's preference for the product, their desire to do or buy more and most intriguingly, their own self-confidence for having chosen to do business with that company in the first place.

Their research indicates that *"82 percent of customers scoring service interactions high on Value Enhancement stayed with that company, 85 percent chose to buy even more and 97 percent recommended that supplier to others."*

Value is the one thing that can persuade your customer to agree with the suggestions that you are about to make.[1]

Before looking at some possible suggestions that can be made in the Discover, Value Alignment and Close sales phases, we will move across to the right-hand side of the FWIN clipboard. The

---

[1]   *Adamson, B. (2020). Customer Service's New Role: Value Enhancement. Retrieved 22 August 2021*

reason we put Value to the right of the FWIN Clipboard is because, in the western world, we scribe from left to right. When populating the clipboard with a customer, it's also a good idea to use positive colors, like blue and green.

Your customer – knowingly or not – is already on a 'Value Scale' with the products and services that they currently use.

Your goal is to convince them that your suggestions will take them closer to achieving their Ultimate Success Outcome.

Here are some typical examples of what we mean by a Value Scale

» *"We are increasingly seeing customers transition from a reactive maintenance approach toward a more proactive method of running their business."*

» *"Where do you see yourself regarding your office heating solution? We see customers moving from gas, oil and mains electric to solar and wind."*

For a more in-depth look at how to build and use the Value Scale on the FWIN clipboard, please check out chapter 3.

Most customers have already deployed solutions to support their Drivers and address their Challenges. Following the Inside Track – and using the FWIN Clipboard – you will be able to gauge where they stand.

This is the perfect moment to share a story of how a customer in a similar situation benefited greatly from moving up the Value Scale. You can describe how that customer ultimately focused their investment on their Drivers and addressed their Challenges. Your customer might be open to a suggestion on how they will benefit from gaining optimum value for their investment.

Some customers already get a high degree of value from their current provider and there is little additional value you can provide. If this is genuinely the case, then it is a good time to move your energy and attention to a customer who will benefit from the value you provide.

Let's look at how you use **Suggest** in more depth in the three Sales Phases.

Suggest for a Discovery call

While preparing for this call, you will have already thought about what you would like to 'Suggest' the actions that you and the customer will subsequently take.

Remember, early in the sales cycle you are looking to balance the suggestion of an immediate solution with a more tentative consultative approach. This opens the way for your potential customer to ask more about your solution.

During the Discovery sales phase it is perfectly reasonable to:

» Show how your products helped other customers to address their drivers and challenges. To achieve this, you may wish to suggest a visit for your prospect to meet an existing, satisfied customer who initially experienced similar challenges.

» Arrange a meeting with the end user in the customer's company to show them the benefits of an investment in your product or service.

» Send out a survey to potential users.

» Speak with other customer stakeholders (and even their customers) to confirm their needs.

» Invest in a pilot project together.

Bear in mind that every potential customer speaks to you with the expectation of finding Value for themselves. Any suggestion you make must demonstrate the Value of committing to taking that step with you and your company.

From your Discovery call, you will learn what the customer considers to be their Ultimate Success Outcome and their perception of value.

For example, in a hospital, you may have 'Optimized Patient Experience' as the Ultimate Success Outcome for the IT department. This might involve a solution whereby all systems talk to each other seamlessly and up-to-date information is available at all levels.

During a Discovery call, you could explain how hospitals are moving from point solutions to a fully integrated Hospital Information Management System. Along the Value Scale, you would list point solutions as Basic Value and integrated systems that simplify hospital operations as the middle. Integrated operational and administrative systems that streamline the process for doctors, nurses and administrators would then go at the top of your Value Scale.

Next, you would talk through the different levels of the Value Scale with your client and work with them to establish where they think they are at on the Value Scale. In the Discovery sales phase, try to stay on the conceptual level, rather than detailing any potential solutions based on your products and services. Your focus is to discover where the customer stands at this point.

By sharing stories of clients who were in a similar position, you will help your customer to see where they fit into the story that evolves in front of them and how you can be useful in helping them to make the best decision for their situation.

At this point, you might also be able to show both qualitative (emotional / intangible) value as well as some quantitative (numerical / tangible) value, based on the information already provided or based on your insight into their industry.

Suggest for an Alignment call

An Alignment call is about getting the different stakeholders and influencers in your customer's organization on your side. Your goal is to find Value for each one of these influencers. If we stay with the previous example of the 'Optimized Patient Experience' as the Ultimate Success Outcome, the people we might now need to align with are perhaps a second or even a third person.

Imagine in this scenario that the first customer you spoke to is the hospital's Chief Information Officer. Your next call with this customer might be with the head of nursing or administration.

Whether Alignment calls are held between the seller and several influencers together or in individual meetings, you will need to return to the earlier chevrons on the Inside Track to gather more information. This is so that you bring in their support in your journey towards closing the deal.

During the Alignment call you can suggest:

» How the Quantitative Value and Qualitative Value benefit each of the stakeholders/influencers you meet.

» Exploring how individual perception of Value fits into optimum value. By doing so, each person sees how the purchase helps move toward the optimum situation for the business.

» Meeting with another influencer to compare their needs.

» How you will represent them in meetings with other influencers.

» That they support you in other internal meetings they have on this topic.

As the dialogue progresses with several stakeholders, Alignment requires you to have more facts and figures to help decision makers justify the investment they make. This situation very often calls for more quantitative value and less on qualitative value.

Just as in your Discovery call, after explaining the Value Scale and how you have drawn it based on independent information from the market, you can simply ask your prospect where they think they fit on the scale in their current situation. After sharing a real customer story, you will then also be able to ask where they would like to be on the scale.

Ultimately, this lets you offer your opinion and to suggest your next steps together.

Suggest for a Closing call

In the Closing sales phase, you will be suggesting that your customer signs a contract with you. How you present your solution to the decision maker(s) is key to holding their attention.

As a short review of the steps explained in the closing call preparation we suggest using the following structure to present your solution:

1. **A bold statement gets attention:**
   A bold statement keeps the audience listening and anticipating an explanation as you talk through your presentation.

2. Reiterate the client's main goals to demonstrate 'we understand you':

Your Solution reflects the customer's Ultimate Success Outcome. It describes how you can help the customer move from their current to their desired situation. This is articulated by avoiding jargon and acronyms and instead by using vocabulary which your customer finds familiar, i.e. their language.

3. Your solution, described in the client's language:

Be short and specific and be sure to leave out any of your own company's abbreviations or acronyms. If any specific vocabulary is used here than it should be the customer's. Almost like name dropping, finding the connection between your solution and any existing customer project names will be more impactful.

4. Quantitative Value quantified in time and money:

This will comprise of:

» Information given to you by past customers.

» Customer satisfaction research conducted by your own company.

» Information captured on your FWIN clipboard, provided by your customer.

All this combined will help you to build a cost benefit analysis that is clear for your customer to align with.

5. Relevant reference cases to demonstrate 'it already works':

Story sharing is a powerful and authentic way to demonstrate your passion and belief that the solution that you are suggesting is tried and tested. A story confirms that what you are proposing is already helping other clients to achieve the same or similar Ultimate Success Outcome. Stories also demonstrate to your customer that partnering with you will achieve the same for them.

6. Why choose you and your company?

The credibility you deliver in this part of your suggestion needs to focus on the unique aspects of you and your company. Remember, something which one customer agrees is unique might be different to the other. Having an in-depth understanding of your local market and your customer's situation will help you to understand and therefore communicate, your unique Value statement. It is useful to look back at the FWIN Clipboard and see what you noted regarding People, Process, Technology and Success Factors, to tailor your message.

7. Next steps to achieve your client's goals:

This involves an explicit request for the customer to sign a contract and to work with you on a time schedule during the coming weeks or months.

Now that we have **Suggested** potential solutions, we can move on to the **Confirm** chevron.

Confirm

In a conversation that has flowed well and in which there are no further questions or concerns, the Confirm element of the Inside Track usually involves agreeing that the mutual expectations from the A.C.E introduction have been achieved. This also includes a summary of the conversation and clarification on the next steps, with which both seller and buyer agree.

If Confirm becomes Concern

Not every sales conversation runs as smoothly as this and the customer may have **questions, objections,** or **concerns.** We prefer to use the term 'Client Concern' to cover all three of these.

In the first instance, let us explore why you need to welcome customer concerns as early as possible in the sales process and why must you face them.

A **customer concern** should be dealt with as soon as it is identified. It may have been put there on purpose (as a tactic used to negotiate) or it might just be misinformation that has caused the client to slow down or even to put a stop to the buying decision. When a customer voices a concern that remains unresolved, the client carries this with them throughout the sales process. Not addressing it immediately guarantees that you will have the concern only reappear later down the line. In the worst-case scenario, this concern may re-appear when the contract is about to be signed. Consequently, instead of signing with you, the client signs with a competitor, leaving you to wonder why this happened. If you do not resolve a client's concerns, then somebody else (usually a competitor) will.

In summary

A repeatable and yet flexible structure will help you to do all the things that are needed to be:

Structured, Confident, Collaborative, Knowledgeable, Competent and In Control.

1. Prepare – to be aware of possible USO and therefore find a C.A.R
2. Introduce - A.C.E
3. Ask Listen Record – D.R.I.V.E - B.R.A.K.E
4. Suggest – influence next step
5. Confirm – mutual expectations reached

The Inside Track is exactly that!

It helps you to Ask, Listen and Record exclusive customer insight, while assembling the wheels of relationship to help people buy from people (that they trust and value).

The human response to resistance

It is common for an emotionally charged situation to arise when a client expresses a concern. The client may change their behavior, which can in turn trigger the salesperson into a defensive or avoidant response. It may also be useful to understand that, just as a buyer can get annoyed with a salesperson trying to sell them something they do not need, so too can a seller feel attacked – or even insulted – when told by a prospective buyer that their offer is of little value.

Some sellers try to avoid objections by changing the subject and hoping they will go away. Others will defend their offering by arguing or trying to persuade the potential client that they are wrong.

Both reactions are in line with natural human behavior commonly known as the 'Fight or Flight' response. The limbic (the oldest part of our brain's evolution) reacts in the same way as an animal would if in danger.

How do you notice these responses in yourself?

You are most likely very familiar with the fight or flight response. Your heartbeat increases and you may begin to feel angry or afraid. When we place this into the context of a sales situation, the natural reaction is to argue or defend your offering (fight) or to ignore (flight) the objection.

Only you have the power to choose your response and therefore your behavior. It just takes practice in noticing your inner dialogue, taking a deep breath and deciding on the response that best serves you, your company and your client.

'Perceived' resistance from a potential customer can happen at any time, from the very first moment you attempt to make contact, right up to the final negotiation. How you conduct yourself when experiencing such perceived resistance can be the difference between making a sale or losing the client.

We have used the word 'perceived' here for good reason. In so many cases, the client is not resisting, even if it sounds a bit like that. Customers are often expressing a concern. However, the potential emotions triggered in you because of what you may see, hear and feel can trigger a defensive behavior. It is useful to note that client concerns are never personal and almost always happen.

Why do customers object?

Why do potential customers object to what you are saying or to what you are selling? Do you recognize any of the following statements?

> *"I don't need what you are selling."*
>
> *"I don't see the value (i.e., the price is greater than the value offered)."*
>
> *"I don't understand what this product will do for me."*
>
> *"I don't have the money."*
>
> *"I am uncertain about hidden costs."*
>
> *"I really don't know what I want."*

You most likely you have answers to combat these statements, that prove the buyer is mistaken. However, if you move directly into combat mode and try to give answers immediately, your customer will feel that you are defending, and you run the risk of ruining the relationship. If you ignore them, the resistance is simply temporarily buried to rise again later.

Very often, customers voice their concerns towards the end of a meeting, and dealing with such concerns is a normal part of any salesperson's daily work. Throughout these discussions where concerns are voiced, we find it beneficial to abide by two golden rules:

1. Avoid 'resistance' by using the D.R.I.V.E method explained in the Ask, Listen, Record section. When a customer is given the opportunity to talk freely about their situation, issues raised can be addressed before they grow into real concerns.

2. Erase the term *'objection'* from your own vocabulary. The term itself is quite negative and it often evokes an equally negative, aggresive, or defensive response. Such a response is the result of the natural fight or flight response mecahnism, the same as when an animal senses danger, we subconsiously prepare to combat or run away from the customers *objection.* When you re-frame it as a 'client concern', you immediately notice the way in which you relate to and deal with the client shifts. Your natural response is then to try and help the customer.

An even more useful way to think about client concerns is to consider this: without concerns your customer would order and arrange delivery themselves without the need for you at all! Essentially, this means that concerns are your gateway into a sale.

The model below will allow you to resolve concerns and help you to build a high level of rapport and trust with your client, who in turn is likely to be grateful for your helpful and valuable explanations.

The R.A.C.E acronym will remind you of the four simple steps which you can take to skillfully handle customer concerns and turn them into a major advantage for you in the process.

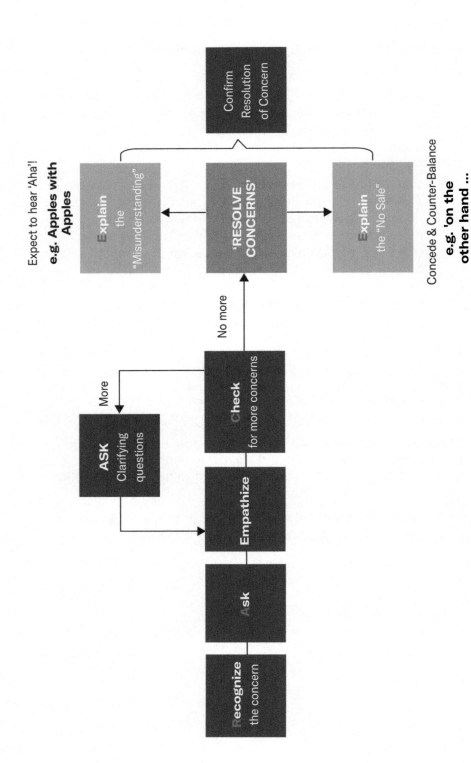

Recognize

Recognize that this is a 'concern' and manage your mental and emotional state. As the fight, flight or freeze reaction potentially kicks in, you will recognize it happening. The skin on your face might become warmer, you might begin to feel tense, perhaps a negative internal dialogue begins to warn you that you are about to lose the sale.

This is the time to take control, to take a deep breath and relax in the knowledge that by following the steps of the R.A.C.E model, you will have alleviated your client's concern.

Take stock of your typical reactions:

» How do you feel when a potential client objects to your offer?

» Is your internal dialogue warning you of an impending danger?

» What do you imagine the customer's mood is when they voice their concern(s)?

» Does your heartbeat increase?

» What is the temperature of your face? Do you get warmer, or does it stay the same?

» Who talks the most in your dialogue with the customer?

Ask

Ask questions to help you both understand why the client is concerned.[1]

Ask your client what makes them feel concerned. Show true empathy as you listen to what they have to say and explore with more questions until you fully understand their concerns. The key at this stage is to listen to why the client is thinking the way they do. If you answer a client's concern with a solution, you signal to them that you did not listen.

---

1   Adamson, B. (2020). Customer Service's New Role: Value Enhancement. Retrieved 22 August 2021

By comparison, refraining from offering solutions and instead seeking to understand by asking relevant questions, you learn why the client is voicing their concern or feelings. Then, you have the opportunity to diffuse a customer's potential fear, anger or anxiety.

You can ask Discover (open) questions to find out:

» Why the customer feels like this?
» What makes them say what they are saying?
» If there is a perfect solution, what would it be?

As you talk, you can collect information on any additional concerns that might arise.

When you have asked enough questions to truly understand your customer's thinking, then (and only then) can you say, 'I understand'. If you do not genuinely understand, you run the risk of losing the trust and rapport you have built up to this point. Saying that you understand does not necessarily mean that you agree. It means that knowing what you know about the situation now allows you to understand the customer's position.

Check

Check that there are no other concerns. After understanding and being able to empathize with the client's concern, it's time to check and see if this is the only concern. If we just resolve the specific concern at hand, then another concern might arise later, and we have to go through the whole process again. Since so-called 'concerns' can sometimes be negotiating tactics, it's vital that we remove them from the conversation so that they don't cause any challenges in the future.

Proper checks will reveal if:

» The client has had a better offer.
» Who the better offer is from.

» Whether the client is 'comparing apples with apples'. By this we mean, does a potentially competing offer contain the same quality or vital feature that your offer does? Perhaps there is some information that the client is unaware of which you can provide.

Once you are sure that you fully understand the client's concerns, you are ready to decide how you will resolve them. You will choose to take one of two directions, as shown in the following 'Apples with Apples' diagram.

Explain 1: Misunderstanding

 Did you know that 70% of all client concerns are caused by misunderstandings? When you list the client concerns that you are likely to face, you will find that they fall into one of three categories, all of which can all be resolved using 'Explain Misunderstanding':

1. Price: Misunderstandings make it necessary to use the 'apples with apples' metaphor. The client learns something about your offering that they didn't know before. You are likely to hear the client saying, 'Aha' as the misunderstanding is cleared up, and the relative merit of your products and solution is revealed. Delaying when you clear up misunderstandings with this metaphor is key. This is because you may already know about the need for an 'apples with apples' comparison at the beginning of your conversation. However it's still necessary for you to go through the whole R.A.C.E process so that you can listen to your client and build rapport.

2. Doubt: Share a true story of how you have helped a client in a similar situation. If it can work for them it can work for you too.

3. Procrastination: Explain why any delay in taking this decision will adversely affect your client's Ultimate Success Outcome. Again share a real account of other clients who have been negatively impacted by delaying a decision to invest in your solution.

Explain 2: 'No Sale'

If you realize that you are not able to beat your competitor's offer (e.g., on price) then you can concede by admitting it! Of course, this is only the beginning. By conceding, you can then counterbalance your apparent defeat by explaining the merits of still doing business with your company. Such a justification might be based on positive past experiences of reliability and satisfaction, or perhaps on a newfound confidence in the future availability of after-sales service.

Your price remains the same, however your important counterarguments give your potential buyer **good reason to reconsider your offer**, as you represent the best solution for their challenges in the long run. Indeed, they may use this final 'counter-balancing' of information to persuade their manager to increase the budget.

 **Practice using R.A.C.E**

Write down your worst 'customer concern', providing as much detail as you can. Feel free to choose one of the examples we have listed in the bullet points below. Be sure to capture 'why' this is a concern to you and what your responses might be.

Practice using R.A.C.E to respond to the following client concerns:

'I can't afford it.'

'I really don't like it.'

'I don't have the authority to buy it.'

'I am afraid of buying the wrong solution.'

'I neither trust, nor believe you.'

'I am not confident you can deliver.'

'I just signed a multi-year contract with your competitor.'

'I don't want to change my way of doing things.'

'I am 100% satisfied with my current supplier.'

'I dislike salespeople in general.'

'I am prejudiced against your company.'

'I need to think about it.'

Plan your difficult customer conversation in full detail below:

Notes
Recognise
Ask
Check
Explain 1:
Explain 2:

In summary

Resolve customer concerns R.A.C.E

A step-by-step approach to helping customers resolve their concerns.

The Human Response to resistance

Fight, Flight or Freeze response

Reframe aggressive objections as genuine concerns that make you want to help

- » Recognize
- » Ask
- » Check
- » Explain

A seller's job is to help clients 'resolve their concerns.' If there were no such 'temporary roadblocks,' then there would be no need for any sales staff at all. Customers would simply look in a catalogue or on the Internet to order and arrange delivery. Sales professionals provide value by dealing with such obstacles in a way that helps the customer feel confident to make the necessary investment.

Conclusion

Do you remember we introduced you to Julie in the Introduction? Before learning the techniques we have presented to you in this book, Julie felt out of her depth as a salesperson; she was demotivated and struggling to meet her targets. By putting theory into practice, Julie went on to achieve incredible success in her role. Every two years, Julie comes back to the Formula Win Training Academy to refresh her skills and maintain her Professional Salesperson Accreditation.

The Inside Track has introduced you to strategies designed to enhance your success at what we call the 'sharp' end of selling. By this, of course, we mean customer interactions and everything that goes along with building relationships and closing deals. Having read it, you now have all of the tools and techniques at your disposal to do the same. Nothing is stopping you from achieving success and enjoying meaningful relationships with your customers.

But before you go...

If there is anything that we hope you take away from this book, it is that the FWIN methodology only works when used in real-life sales scenarios. Having read this far, if you plan to close the book and put it on your shelf, we urge you to stop and consider doing something different.

Place this book on your desk where you can see it, or in your work bag. We've consciously chosen to create a small and light book for you to carry around with you, so don't let it become another of those dusty tomes on your shelf that gets enjoyed but forgotten.

Our mission is for The Inside Track to become your trusted go-to companion that you can pick up, open on any page and refresh yourself on what you've learned. Even by opening on a random page before you head into a customer meeting, you will be reminded of a gem of knowledge or a nugget of information that can help you move closer to closing the deal.

What else can you do right now to ensure your ongoing success?

Before returning to 'life as normal', give yourself an hour and think about how you will do things differently from now on. Perhaps make yourself a coffee and if it's a nice day, take some reflection time outside to consolidate your learning.

In our experience, this is the part that most people miss when it comes to changing habits or learning new skills.

Perhaps take some time to consider your Sparks or make contact with your co-driver to set up a meeting for the week ahead. Plan in regular check-ins with this person for the next six months and commit to the times, even if you have a lot going on.

You might want to look back over the notes you've made or even flick through the chapter headings and the main models, such as D.R.I.V.E, A.C.E or B.R.A.K.E How will you implement these into your day? Can you identify a way that you might use them in your next phone call with a customer? Set reminders on your phone if you feel this is something that will help you.

The key here is to spend the time considering what is going to work for YOU. You know yourself better than anyone, and so if you have a preferred way of setting yourself reminders or you know something has worked well for you in the past, use that approach.

Further resources

Join our Facebook community by searching for *Formula Win Selling* or visit www.formulawinselling.com to watch our range of sales training videos.

On our website, you can also book a coaching call with Andy to refine your skills and check out anything you may want to discuss in more detail. Many of our readers and workshop participants have found that ***one-to-one coaching*** can help consolidate their learning and clear up any queries.

The website also provides details of future book releases, including *The Qualifying Lap, Winning the Circuit* leading to *The Finish Line.*

Stay in touch

We'd love to hear your feedback and success stories. When you have implemented the learning and are ready to share how things are going with you, drop us a line at moresales@formulawinselling.com.

We hope to hear from you! But in the meantime...

Thank you for reading this book. We wish you success and prosperity in your sales activities

Andy and Beat

Appendix
Turning Learning into Practice
'MAKING NEW HABITS STICK'

All the knowledge in this and in the abundance of other personal and professional development books is of little value if we do not put the learning, at least partially, into practice.

At Formula Win Selling face-to-face and online training sessions, we regularly receive feedback from salespeople telling us that the skills they learned are so valuable and so useful that they will put them into practice as soon as they get back to work. Then what happens?

Well, life gets in the way, that's what happens, and they forget! The reality is that even when we truly WANT to put the new learning into practice, making it a new habit is not that easy. Well, it wasn't that easy, until now!

I'm sure you will agree that the way to make learning valuable is to make it a habit. Since ancient times, human beings have sought to purposely change their behavior, so it becomes automatic. It is this automaticity that makes skillful performance look so easy. Just take a moment to imagine any top sports person, musician or sales professional at work – looks easy, doesn't it? Why? Because they learned, they practiced and then they turned that practice into a habit. As Aristotle said, *"We are the sum of our actions: therefore, our habits make all the difference."*

After years of grappling with the age-old adage, *"You can take a horse to water but you can't make it drink!"*, we have taken what we know from our experience and from the most practicable habit-forming research to offer you a way of turning our winning formula into your winning habit.

To purposely form habits, many of us leave ourselves notes or even strategically place objects on the bedroom floor, such as a pair of running shoes, to remind us of the habit we would like to form.

This concept of placing reminders where you will see them is not new. If you have ever wanted to learn a new language, perhaps you have put sticky notes in that language on objects around your house to remind you of the new vocabulary? How many of us have, at school, jotted down a key word or two on a ruler or pencil case to remind us of that vital link needed to solve a common physics question? Some called it cheating, Andy called it his 'spark'.

Sparks

Such visual reminders fall under a category of tool we purposely use at Formula Win Selling called 'Sparks'. Just as sparkplugs have, for many years, ignited fuel in our cars to get us moving - FWIN sparks ignite a specific action or technique when selling. They can be anything from a note on your car dashboard reminding you to take a sample to the customer, to letters on your gear-shift reminding you of a specific Formula Win acronym.

Several visual and auditory 'sparks' in your car prompt you to carry out performance-enhancing actions as you work with concepts in the book. For example, when you see your gear-shift, you imagine the letters D.R.I.V.E in place of the numbers and this reminds you of a key FWIN acronym used when questioning customers. On the other hand, your fuel and temperature gauges remind you to think of your physical and mental health (vital for the wellbeing of any person working in sales). The fuel reminds you of the food you ate today, the temperature gauge of your emotional state before entering a meeting.

Such reminders need not be only visual; they can be auditory or even olfactory (using smells), e.g., a sound from your smartphone, a song which helps you enter a different mental state, such as the tune from the film 'Rocky' for energy or a calmer tune to prepare you for a customer who is also calm by nature.

The renaming of your favorite radio station on your car radio screen as 'CRM 1' or 'FWIN CIRCUIT' is an instant spark that prevents you from driving away from a customer until you have finished filling out the crucial details of your customer meeting in your notebook or online CRM platform.

As mentioned above, sparks can also be olfactory. The ability to smell is still a primate sense that alerts the brain directly and without any learned filtering. What if the cologne or perfume you choose could remind you to listen more intently or to ask specific, rapport-building questions of your customer? You can arrange this by anchoring the aroma to a positive experience when such great listening helped you to close a sale.

As someone who wants to form new habits, you are in control. All it takes is a purposeful approach to putting new behaviors into practice. However, we are aware that not one size fits all and after experimentation, you will be able to choose the habit-forming method that works best for you.

If you find that the traditional use of reminders tends to wear off, one reason could be that an important element is missing in the process – there is no 'immediate' reward.

The 3 Ps - Provoke - Perform - Prize

Right the way back to experiments performed by the Russian physiologist Ivan Pavlov in the 1890s, we have known that it is not difficult to instill automatic behaviors in animals, such as by ringing a bell and rewarding the animal with food, so that they are keen to repeat the process next time.

It can be said that many human habits – both good and bad – are formed in a similar way to those of Pavlov's dogs when an event acts as a reminder that 'provokes' a response. Some people need only smell coffee in the air, and they are immediately compelled to light up a cigarette. Others hear a specific catchy tune and start to hum, tap, or even sing along to it. As we have seen, the phenomenon of habits is not new and yet it could be used so much more to our advantage if we could only use this knowledge to purposely guarantee the use of positive habits in our personal and professional lives.

Formula Win Selling success relies heavily on you turning the sales techniques into everyday habits. We believe that a combination of the 'visual sparks' mentioned earlier and the concept of 'Anchor Moments' from a methodology invented by Behavior Scientist Dr. BJ Fogg to be the magic formula that will help you to put FWIN selling techniques into practice with your customers.

Tiny Habits – small changes that change everything

This book is full of strategies, techniques, methods that are composed of actions/behaviors that we ultimately want to become habits. We chose a methodology that we know works as we have used it ourselves from a number of years. The success behind the concept of 'Tiny Habits' lies in the fact that they are tiny! Each new behavior may not take more than 30 seconds to practice from your busy day.

Some examples might be: to read one paragraph of a book or to do one push up – they are that tiny!

They other key factor is that the prompt is not a spark (visual or otherwise) but an existing behavior that Dr BJ Fogg calls an *Anchor Moment*. This can be anything from getting out of bed (a behavior we hope you follow every morning) to pouring a cup of coffee.

Leverage existing habits 'Anchor Moments'

You already have many good (and bad) well-established habits that you carry out every day, if not multiple times per day. The 'Tiny Habits' methodology mentioned above benefits from using such habits known as *Anchor Moments* as a springboard to performing a new desired habit. These 'anchor moments' are existing habitual actions that once identified can be used to stimulate the new behavior that you would like to follow.

To remind you of the Formula Win habit you would like to repeat, we suggest using a combination of 'visual sparks' mostly found in your car and The Tiny Habits *Anchor Moments*. You are of course free to choose the best method that suits you, your needs and your context. For example, it may happen that in some scenarios it's not possible to prepare or even to use an overt visual or auditory spark. In such circumstances, the most reliable and effective way to embed that habitual action will be to rely on the Tiny Habits method, using visual 'sparks' as a backup if possible or if necessary.

A new habit in 30 seconds!

The good news, and music to salespeoples' ears is that training 'Tiny Habits' can be done very quickly.

Rather than launching into Tiny Habits for work scenarios immediately, we suggest applying them for personal use first. Then when you see how easy they are to make use of at home, you can begin to adapt the methodology to the techniques in the book with your customers.

You will immediately notice that the actual new habit is truly 'tiny'. In fact, it is something you 'must' do in less than 30 seconds. This ensures you not only have the ability to do it but that any resistance is hugely reduced. These habits do start tiny but as you experience later, you will soon start to gain 'extra credits' and the new habits very often become life-changing!

Simple instructions to practice 'Tiny Habits'

After you have chosen your 'Desired New Habit' the process is as simple as A-B-C

    A. Anchor moment - Choose an EXISTING ACTION that you do every day. (Anchor Moment) such as brushing your teeth.

    B. Behavior – Choose the new (tiny) habit that you would like to begin doing.

    C. Remember, the behavior should take no more than 30 seconds. After 'ANCHOR MOMENT', do your NEW (Tiny) HABIT.

    D. Celebration – research shows that this memorable act encourages you to repeat the habit in the future. So think of a way that you can celebrate. Be bold! This works really well if it is memorable, emotional or simply loud! (we would like to get the positive effects of neurotransmitters such as dopamine and adrenaline pumping through your body) The following examples are written in the same way as you will write them down yourself in your own Tiny Habits 'recipes'. We have also added possible reminders marked with an *asterisk should you find the need for them.

Four example 'recipes' for habitual success:

1. *Desired new Habit: Increase my fitness.*

   A. *Anchor moment (spark):* Brushing your teeth

   B. *Behavior/New Habit:* After replacing my toothbrush, I will do 3 push-ups everyday.

   *If you find yourself forgetting, why not reinforce the memory jogger by writing on the toothbrush or draw a symbol, e.g., three push-ups.... or choose a more powerful anchor moment.

   C. *Celebrate:* After doing 3 push-ups, I will gargle loudly with fresh, cold water to celebrate.

2. *Desired new Habit: Improve my relationship.*

   A. *Anchor moment (spark)*: Hearing your alarm clock.

   B. *Behavior/New Habit*: After waking up to the sound of my alarm, I will make two cups of tea every day.

   *If you forget, why not change the smartphone alarm clock ring tone with a recording of your voice or of the song 'Tea for Two'. Make 'two' cups of tea and transform your relationship day by day. .... or choose a more powerful anchor moment.

   C. *Celebrate:* As I lift up my cup to take the sip, I will say 'cheers' to my life partner.

3. *Desired new Habit: 'Read' more books.*

   A. *Anchor moment (spark):* Putting on your seatbelt in the car.

   B. *Behavior/New Habit*: After fastening my seatbelt and when I hear that 'click', I will switch on my audiobook connected to the car infotainment system.

   C. *Celebrate:* Then I will celebrate with an almighty 'Hallelujah' (you're in the car, no one will hear you).

4. **Desired new Habit: Put myself into the right frame of mind/mood before visiting a customer.**

    A. **Anchor moment (spark)**: Turning the key to switch off the car engine.

    B. **Behaviour/New Habit:** After turning off the car engine (when I arrive at the customer's office), I will play the chosen song that takes me back to a specific experience when I felt 'strong', empathic', 'joyful' and 'relaxed'.

        *If you tend to forget or as a visual backup you can add a removable 'Smilie' sticker to your car dashboard, or choose a more powerful anchor moment.

        *Less than a minute can be enough before leaving your car to visit a customer. Those few seconds could make all the difference.

    C. **Celebrate** by punching the air and saying to yourself, 'YES .. GOOD JOB' (before leaving the car).

For these habits, you will need to pre-program a memorable song, accessed at the simple touch of a button (it must be easy to do) into your car playlist to play.

When sparks work and when they don't work so well!

Andy's personal reasons for referring to Dr BJ Fogg's model as opposed to others is that after practicing it for more than two years, the realization was that a SPARK (or as BJ calls it, 'the prompt/anchor moment') is simply not enough. One must also consider the critical factors of Motivation and Ability. The Behavior model on the next page was created by BJ in 2007 at Stanford University illustrates this perfectly.

Motivation and Ability are crucial in making the 'spark' effective. Only when we have the ingredients of Motivation (M) and Ability (A) present in the correct quantity, do we react to the Spark/Prompt/Anchor moment (P) in the way that we desire.

As Dr Fogg's formula shows Behavior $= M + A + P$

You can read more about this phenomenon and a more detailed account of the process described here at www.bjfogg.com, where you can also order the book.

Dr Fogg's behavior model, illustrated above, clearly shows that the

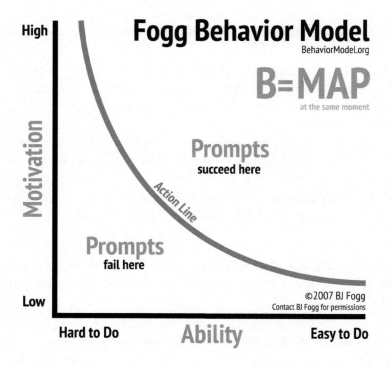

prompt/SPARK (anchor moment) must appear above the action line! It cannot be more difficult than your perceived ability and you must be 'motivated enough' to want to undertake the new behavior (in the case of FWIN, a new sales technique).

The buddy system of Pitstops

At the end of each chapter in this book, we suggest that you will meet with your most influential and important spark - your 'co-driver'. i.e. a colleague/friend who is also following the book and is also trying out the Pitstop exercises.

To remember to do this, you can even put a photo of your co-driver on your car dashboard if you like. (We are sure your life partner will understand!) Alternatively, why not find an existing anchor moment that normally occurs when you speak with each other.

We are sure you will agree that all the tasks (pit stops) in this book are, in fact, within your and your co-driver's Ability. That leaves the question of motivation. Why do you want to make this new selling technique a habit? Ultimately; why do you want to improve your current sales performance? How high is your motivation?

The Tiny Habits model recognizes that Motivation is not the only key to habit-forming but that it can move up and down like the tide. Knowing this allows you to design a 'recipe' (like one of the four examples in previous pages) that not only reduces the difficulty of the task enough to force the new behavior above the action line but that you are clear about your motivation to carry out the task.

In the case shown in the graph above, you increase your ability by doing four push-ups instead of a hundred. In terms of motivation you might want to think of your personal motivation of looking good, your ideas of 'What's in It for You' – benefit or punishment (carrot/stick) reason for doing it and also your environment for doing it. Is your new habit possible/acceptable in that scenario?

Extra Credits

In reality, what often happens is, as these Tiny Habits become embedded, the 'Habiteer' adds to the task. Even though this gains 'extra credits', as BJ calls them, the simple task of 4 push-ups remains the desired new behavior. For example, Andy does 60 push-ups every morning – he says it gets the adrenaline flowing and switches on his brain to a positive mindset. BJ reminds him that his goal is still only 4! (and congratulates him on his 56 extra credits!)

Which 'sparks' or 'anchor moments' will you use to form the habits of using A.C.E, D.R.I.V.E, BREAK and R.A.C.E?

References

Adamson, B. (2020). Customer Service's New Role: Value Enhancement. Retrieved 22 August 2021, from https://www.destinationcrm.com/ Articles/Web-Exclusives/Viewpoints/Customer-Services-New-Role-Value-Enhancement-144125.aspx

Angevine, C., Plotkin, C. L., & Stanley, J. (2017). When B2B buyers want to go digital–and when they don't. McKinsey Quarterly, 8, 12-15. https://www.mckinsey.de/~/media/McKinsey/Business%20Functions/ McKinsey%20Digital/Our%20Insights/When%20B2B%20buyers%20 want%20to%20go%20digital%20and%20when%20they%20dont/ When-B2B-buyers-want-to-go-digital-and-when-they-dont.pdf

Coch, D., Sanders, L. D., and Neville, H. J. (2005). An event-related potential study of selective auditory attention in children and adults. J. Cogn. Neurosci. 17, 605–622. https://direct.mit.edu/jocn/ article/17/4/605/3995/An-Event-related-Potential-Study-of-Selective

Demand Gen Report (2016). 2016 Content Preferences Survey: B2B Buyers Value Content That Offers Data And Analysis. Retrieved 22 August 2021, from
https://www.demandgenreport.com/resources/research/2016-content-preferences-survey-b2b-buyers-value-content-that-offers-data-and-analysis/
You can also read about these findings here: https://earnest-agency. com/ideas-and-insight/the-only-b2b-statistics-youll-ever-need-plus-a-few-shockers/

Demand Gen Report (2018). 2018 Content Preferences Survey Report. Retrieved 22 August 2021, from
https://www.demandgenreport.com/resources/research/2018-content-preferences-survey-report/

Hart, R. (2017). Customers need a reason to remember you. Forrester. Retrieved 22 August 2021, from https://www.forrester.com/report/ Customers+Need+A+Reason+To+Remember+You/RES137182

James, A., Narus, J., & van Rossum, W. (2006). Customer value propositions in business markets. Harvard Business Review, 84(3), 1-10.

You can read the paper here: https://e-tarjome.com/storage/btn_
uploaded/2020-10-20/1603172544_11424-etarjome%20English.pdf

Newman, D. (2015). Love It Or Hate It: Influencer Marketing Works.
Retrieved 22 August 2021, from https://www.forbes.com/sites/
danielnewman/2015/06/23/love-it-or-hate-it-influencer-marketing-
works/#3ea9585a150b

McGinnis, D. (2019). Customer Service Statistics and Trends. Retrieved
22 August 2021, from https://www.salesforce.com/blog/customer-
service-stats/

Nathan, S., & Schmidt, K. (2013). Promotion to Emotion: Connecting B2B
Customers to Brands. Retrieved 22 August 2021, from
https://www.thinkwithgoogle.com/consumer-insights/consumer-trends/
promotion-emotion-b2b/

PwC (2018). Future of Customer Experience Survey 2017/18. PwC.
Retrieved 22 August 2021, from
https://www.pwc.com/us/en/advisory-services/publications/consumer-
intelligence-series/pwc-consumer-intelligence-series-customer-
experience.pdf

Woldorff, M. G., Gallen, C. C., Hampson, S. A., Hillyard, S. A., Pantev,
C., Sobel, D., and Bloom, F. E. (1993). Modulation of early sensory
processing in human auditory cortex during auditory selective
attention. Proc. Natl. Acad. Sci. U.S.A. 90, 8722–8726. https://www.
pnas.org/content/90/18/8722.long

Printed in Great Britain
by Amazon

13145614R00075